Critical Guides to Spanish

C000193610

31 Miguel de Unamuno: San Manuel Bueno, mártir

Critical Guides to Spanish Texts

EDITED BY J. E. VAREY AND A. D. DEYERMOND

MIGUEL DE UNAMUNO

San Manuel Bueno, mártir

John Butt

Lecturer in Spanish
University of London, King's College

Grant & Cutler Ltd *in association with*
Tamesis Books Ltd 1981

© Grant & Cutler Ltd
   1981
ISBN 0 7293 0111 7

I.S.B.N. 84-499-4980-7

DEPÓSITO LEGAL: 2.164 - 1981

Printed in Spain by
Artes Gráficas Soler, S. A. - Olivereta, 28 - Valencia (18)
for
GRANT & CUTLER LTD
11 BUCKINGHAM STREET, LONDON, W.C.2

For Mikko

Contents

Contents

Preface

IN this critical guide I have included a good deal of information about Unamuno's thought and life which I hope will illuminate *San Manuel Bueno, mártir*. I reject the kind of criticism which sticks rigidly to the facts of the text in the belief that they contain everything that can or need be known about it without reference to outside factors. Such an approach usually ends by repeating the fallacies of interpretative criticism: pressing on the reader another subjective, often merely fanciful reading of the sort which abounds in *Unamunismo*. Instead I try to provide a context in which the reader can read and judge the novel for himself.

I also insist heavily on the contradictory quality of Unamuno's thought, and this may be disconcerting. It is hard to resist the entreaties of that imaginary reader, the hard-pressed examinations candidate, for a simplified account of the work which he can adopt as his own. But his pleas must be turned down if one is to do Unamuno anything like justice. It is really not possible to simplify or talk away the ambiguities and inconsistencies in his work, for of all authors he is the most exasperatingly and deliberately contradictory. Even his well-known admiration for the piety and tranquillity of village life has to be set against his support of a hare-brained scheme to marshal the peasantry into large cities on the grounds that this is the only way to civilize them. [1] Much *Unamunismo* glosses over such *non sequiturs* in the interests of clarity, but in doing so it falsifies his work. Instead I try to lay bare the inconsistencies because contradiction and even incoherence is the

[1] 'La civilización es civismo', April 1907, in *OC*, IV, pp. 445-9, at p. 451.

essential quality of Unamuno's thought on the major questions he dealt with, and conflict and contradiction are the source of the ambiguous and in many ways mysterious text of *San Manuel Bueno, mártir*.

Those who are new to Unamuno's work should be wary of drawing too many conclusions about his character or beliefs from *San Manuel Bueno, mártir,* a work which some *Unamunistas* have (for no obvious reason) taken as the definitive final statement of his real views about the matters it raises. To read it thus consigns all his earlier, major works to the status of provisional stages in his thought. There is surely something wrong with a critical approach which takes only the last works in a man's life as the true record of his beliefs.

San Manuel Bueno, mártir in many ways actually negates what Unamuno stood for himself, and my general argument is that it should be read neither as a straight reflection of its author's beliefs nor as an attempt at a realistic portrayal of rural life in the modern age. The novel has a strong element of fantasy, and it is in some ways a tentative, hesitant and what Unamuno would call an exemplary *(ejemplar)* work — i.e. it offers a particular instance or case of human behaviour but in many ways suspends judgement on it.

It seems to me, in fact, that there is a good case for reading it as a religious allegory about the life of Jesus rather than as a human story about a sceptical village priest. If I seem to overdo this allegorical reading it is in part to redress the balance against the psychological or existentialist interpretations which abound in Unamuno studies and concentrate the reader's attention excessively on the surface features of character and plot in the novel.

References

All references to the text of *San Manuel Bueno, mártir* are taken from the eighth Alianza Editorial 'Libro de Bolsillo' edition (Madrid, 1979) on the grounds that this cheap volume is likely to be used by ordinary readers. The quotations have been checked against the text of Mario and María Elena

Valdés, *Comparative and Critical Edition of San Manuel Bueno, mártir,* Estudios de Hispanófila, no. 27 (Chapel Hill, 1973) and discrepancies noted where they occur.

All quotations from Unamuno, except where indicated, are from the *Obras completas,* edited by Manuel García Blanco, 16 vols (Madrid: Afrodisio Aguado, 1958-64), hereinafter referred to as *OC.*

The figures in parentheses in italic type refer to the numbered items in the Bibliographical Note; the italic figure is followed by a page reference.

I am indebted to Ms Isabel Soto for her advice on a number of points.

1. *Introduction*

SAN Manuel Bueno, mártir was written, Unamuno tells us, virtually at a single sitting ('casi de un solo tirón') in November 1930. [1] It was published in magazine form in *La Novela de Hoy* on 13 March 1931, and in book form by Espasa-Calpe in the Summer of 1933: the latter edition included three other short stories and a long prologue, and is still available as the Austral title *San Manuel Bueno, mártir y tres historias más*. There are a number of discrepancies between the manuscript and the first printed edition, and trifling differences between the latter and the 1933 version. These have been noted where necessary. A major innovation in some later editions, including Alianza, is the numbering of chapters, which were indicated in Unamuno's version by simple gaps in the text. This editorial tampering is not without its artistic implications: structurally it alters the novel by converting it from a single, apparently spontaneous, unplanned and necessarily disorganized recollection of Manuel by Angela Carballino, into an ordered, calculated chronicle of events more closely resembling a conventional novel. This decision to number the chapters was (as far as I know) never authorized by Unamuno, and almost certainly thwarts one of his chief intentions in this work — that of presenting the story of Manuel Bueno as a fragment from an individual's memories rather than as a carefully composed and structured work of art.

[1] Prologue to Espasa-Calpe edition of 1933, in *OC*, II, pp. 1181-93, at p. 1184. This prologue is unfortunately omitted from the Alianza edition, but may be read in the Austral paperback edition of *San Manuel Bueno, mártir y tres historias más*, Colección Austral, no. 254 (Buenos Aires, 1942; often reprinted).

The 1931 edition was warmly reviewed by Gregorio Marañón who thought the novel would be one of Unamuno's most popular works. Unamuno was himself aware of the special qualities of the text. In the prologue of 1931 he wrote, 'tengo la conciencia de haber puesto en ella todo mi sentimiento trágico de la vida cotidiana' (*OC,* II, p. 182). Subsequent critics have been virtually unanimous in endorsing his judgement: Marías called it 'la más entrañable y honda novela de Unamuno' (*11,* p. 112), Batchelor claims that it plumbs 'a depth of feeling the other *nivolas* fail to reach' (*17,* p. 69), and Francisco Ayala thought it approached 'lo perfecto desde todos los puntos de vista' (quoted in *18,* p. 247).

The setting was suggested to Unamuno by a visit he made on 1 June 1930 to the lake of Sanabria, a remote beauty spot where, according to a legend which dates back at least 700 years, a village called Villaverde or Valverde de Lucerna or Lucena lies drowned beneath the waters. This village, which has been fairly conclusively identified as the mythical town of Luiserne mentioned in the French epic *Anseïs de Carthage* was, according to a legend apparently still told by local villagers, destroyed by Christ himself who raised a great flood of water when he came to its gates disguised as a beggar and was refused alms. Any person in a state of grace who approaches the lakeside on St John's Day (27 December) is supposed to hear the bell of the submerged church. [2] The idea that Christ himself walked these shores of the lake may have some bearing on the novel (assuming — as we probably may — that Unamuno heard the whole legend).

The lake seems to have impressed him. He wrote two poems which record its impact on him, and both contain allusions to his morbid preoccupation with smooth expanses of water and with oblivion. The first reads:

> San Martín de Castañeda,
> espejo de soledades,

[2] Details from Martín de Riquer, *Los cantares de gesta franceses* (Madrid, 1952), pp. 345-52. I am grateful to Dr David Hook for his help in tracing this legend.

el lago recoge edades
de antes del hombre y se queda
soñando en la santa calma
del cielo de las alturas
en que se sume en honduras
de anegarse, ¿pobre! el alma...
Campanario sumergido
de Valverde de Lucerna,
toque de agonía eterna
bajo el caudal del olvido.
La historia paró al sendero
de San Bernardo, la vida
retorna, y todo se olvida
lo que no fuera primero.

And the second:

Ay, Valverde de Lucerna
hez del lago de Sanabria,
no hay leyenda que dé cabria
de sacarte a luz moderna.
Se queja en vano tu bronce
en la noche de San Juan,
tus hornos dieron su pan,
la historia se está en su gonce.
Servir de pasto a las truchas
es, aun muerto, amargo trago;
se muere Riba de Lago
orilla de nuestras luchas. [3]

Both poems show how Unamuno felt the place to be quite remote from History — 'orilla de nuestras luchas' — and untroubled by contemporary events; in the next chapter we shall see why such isolation and calm might well have attracted him in those days. It is also clear that Valverde de Lucerna immediately fascinated him as a legendary place of death and forgetting. The reader of Unamuno's poetry will know that

[3] *OC*, II, pp. 1182-3. The remains of a monastery of the Cistercian Order (founded by St Bernard) are visible at one end of the lake.

any scene which reminded him of man's eventual fate produced a powerful poetic charge in him.

But we should not think of the Sanabria lake as the direct inspiration of the novel, which was written after a gestation period of some five months. In his prologue of 1933 Unamuno mentions three wretched villages built round the shore of the lake, Riba de Lago, San Martín de la Castañeda and Galande, the first of them a decaying hamlet, its inhabitants destitute. It is tempting to take one of them, particularly Riba de Lago, as the real Valverde de Lucerna, itself built on the lakeside in the novel; but Unamuno is at pains to dispel this notion:

> Ninguno de los tres puede ser ni fue el modelo de mi Valverde de Lucerna. El escenario de la obra de mi Don Manuel Bueno ... supone un desarrollo mayor de vida pública, por pobre y humilde que ésta sea, que la vida de esas pobrísimas y humildísimas aldeas. (*OC,* II, pp. 1183-4)

This is a strange remark. The Valverde de Lucerna in the novel is shown to be quite cut off from contemporary events, apparently ignorant of the social and political problems of the day. It is not clear how the 'greater development of public life' actually manifests itself there. More of this later.

San Manuel Bueno, mártir is in many ways a deceptive text, short and apparently straightforward, but in reality not quite answering to the sort of interpretation that (to judge by some of the critics) a cursory reading provides. Angela Carballino, an aged spinster, is supposed to have written a manuscript which has mysteriously come into Unamuno's hands. It contains her recollections of the pious life and death of Manuel Bueno, the parish priest of Valverde de Lucerna, a shadowy village of obscure location. More precisely, it largely contains her recollections of her brother's revelations about Manuel Bueno: the account is thus filtered through two narrative versions and we get relatively little direct knowledge of the priest's thoughts. Then by the time she has come to write (years after Manuel's death) the priest's reputation has grown so great that the bishop of the diocese has started formalities to have him canonized.

But the Church is, like the ordinary people of Valverde, the victim of a stupendous deception. Before his death Manuel had revealed, first to Angela's brother Lázaro, then through him to her (although Manuel does not care to be too open with her himself) that he does not believe the Church's teaching about an afterlife. (It may be noted here that he does not explicitly deny belief in God; the point will be taken up again.) It is not that Manuel has undergone some change in his beliefs in the past, though critics of the novel constantly talk of 'loss of faith': he never really seems to have had much or any in the first place — a fact which makes his decision to enter the priesthood all the more peculiar. He mentions that there had possibly been a time in his childhood when he had believed in an afterlife, '¡y entonces sí que creía en la vida perdurable! Es decir, me figuro ahora que creía entonces' (p. 65), and we are told that he had first entered a seminary to study for the priesthood not so much from religious conviction as to earn money to keep his widowed sister and her children (p. 12). We are also told nothing about the reasons why he does not believe: he himself does not even try to explain it. Manuel is in fact a mysterious figure. We learn virtually nothing of his origins, his family or background, save that his father was a depressive.

Despite this inauspicious (though charitable) beginning, his subsequent career as a priest is exemplary. Refusing a brilliant ecclesiastical career, he devotes himself to his parishioners who soon sense his peculiar sanctity: 'Empezaba el pueblo a olerle la santidad' (p. 8). His relationship with them is close and practical. He helps them with their work, reconciles estranged couples, finds parents for illegitimate children — indeed he is especially fond of children. His pious reputation is soon so great that the sick come from far and wide in the hope — sometimes rewarded — of miraculous cures (p. 14). His favourites are the poor and unfortunate, especially the village idiot Blasillo who seems to be inspired with intelligence and insights through his care and love. Towards the civil authorities he displays the attitude of Jesus — that public matters are irrelevant to religion. In fact Manuel's Catholicism is quite apolitical: he never rails against Masons, liberals or heretics. A curious feature is his constant activity, as though he were fleeing his private thoughts (p. 19). He encourages laughter and gaiety everywhere, as is shown by his wish that he could turn the lake to wine and by his admiration for the clown. The clown, in fact, fulfils a role similar to Manuel's, entertaining others while he weeps inwardly: he is an effective symbol of the kind of self-abnegation Manuel stands for. Manuel does not care for the monastic life, his whole existence being devoted to others: 'Yo no podría soportar las tentaciones del desierto', he comments meaningfully (p. 27).

Such is the picture that Angela forms of Manuel on her return from the convent in Renada. Her first emotions towards him are a mixture of awe and solicitude: she is deeply touched by his utterance of the words 'My God, my God, wherefore hast thou forsaken me?', and on two occasions she remarks that she looked upon him as a mother upon a son:

> Empezaba yo a sentir una especie de afecto maternal hacia mi padre espiritual; quería aliviarle del peso de su cruz del nacimiento. (p. 34)

> ... y al salir de la iglesia se me estremecían las entrañas maternales. (p. 51)

It is worth noting that these lines were added by Unamuno in the first printed edition of the novel (1931) and do not appear in the manuscript of 1930. Unamuno, whose heroines are nearly always maternal in their attitude towards men, clearly felt a subsequent need to strengthen the emotional involvement of Angela when he came to correct his text. [4] However, the function of chapter III is to show us that in the eight years between her return to Valverde and her brother's arrival from America, she intuited and was drawn by Manuel's mysterious

[4] For a study of the corrections between the manuscript and the editions of 1931 and 1933, see Valdés, *3*, pp. 11-14.

sadness. Her brother's return from America, where he has absorbed a fashionable anti-clericalism, is the occasion for the disclosure of Manuel's dire secret. Lázaro arrives brimming with contempt for the medieval backwardness of the village and the superstitious regard of its inhabitants for don Manuel. But he soon changes his mind on further acquaintance with the priest. It is the experience of death — his mother's — which inspires his conversion, as often in Unamuno's works where realization of the brevity of life is a philosophical turning point for many characters. From anti-clerical progressivism he is rapidly won over to at least an outward show of Catholic piety (p. 43). In a touching scene he condescends to take Communion from Manuel's hand — a sacrilegious act (since he is a non-believer) which he defends on the grounds that it makes everyone happy. Lázaro now becomes Manuel's chief accomplice in deception, and he soon explains the situation to his astonished sister: the priest is merely acting the part of a convinced Christian because he is sure that ordinary men need belief in an afterlife to preserve their *joie de vivre* and to keep at bay the dreadful knowledge of human mortality. Religions are necessary, Manuel says, not because they are true but because they are consoling lies: 'Todas las religiones son verdaderas en cuanto hacen vivir espiritualmente a los pueblos que las profesan' (pp. 46-7).

Manuel makes further melancholy disclosures to Lázaro, who reports them to his sister. Most significant, perhaps, is that Manuel has a death-wish which he supposes inherited from his father and which he sublimates in feverish activity. He confesses that the waters of the lake draw him constantly:

> ¡Y cómo me llama esa agua con su aparente quietud
> — la corriente va por dentro — espeja al cielo! Mi vida,
> Lázaro, es una especie de suicidio continuo, un combate
> contra el suicidio, que es igual ... (p. 53)

Critics have rarely commented on the paradox of this confession of an urge to suicide. It seems odd that a man whose whole philosophy and conduct are based on a deep sadness about human mortality and the finality of death should at the same time be tempted to kill himself. The text of *San Manuel Bueno, mártir* offers no clues as to the reason for these apparently conflicting impulses: we are merely told that the basic cause of Manuel's constant social activities is a desire to escape from his own morbid thoughts. Charity and Christian love are not his only motives for acts of selflessness.

Perhaps we can understand Manuel by reference to his author, even if such explanations can only be speculative. Unamuno was himself tempted from time to time by suicide, and had recently been visited by an unusually strong urge to drown himself when, in 1924, he had become fascinated by the 'mirror' of the waters of the Seine while he was crossing the Pont d'Âme:

> Y cuando ... he atravesado el puente de Alma he sentido ganas de arrojarme al Sena, al espejo. He tenido que agarrarme al parapeto. Y me he acordado de otras tentaciones parecidas, ahora ya viejas, y de aquella fantasía del suicida de nacimiento que imaginé que vivió cerca de ochenta años queriendo siempre suicidarse y matándose por el pensamiento día a día. [5]

It is clear that the life-long candidate for self-destruction whom Unamuno mentions appears in *San Manuel Bueno, mártir* in the shape of Manuel's father whose suicidal urge the priest has inherited (pp. 52-3). The morbid fascination the lake holds for the priest is further explained by other remarks in *Cómo se hace una novela:*

> Cuando, por un instante, separándolos de las páginas del libro, los fija [i.e. his eyes] en las aguas del Sena, paréceles que esas aguas no corren, que son las de un espejo inmóvil y aparta de ellas sus ojos horrorizados ... (p. 867)

This sinister effect of smooth surfaces of water on Unamuno's troubled mind is also connected with his obsession with mirrors. He was apparently incapable of looking at his own image in

[5] *Cómo se hace una novela* (1927), in *OC*, X, pp. 827-926, at pp. 867-8.

a looking-glass: doing so reminded him of the nothingness which lies just beyond all experience —

> Y he aquí por qué no puedo mirarme un rato al espejo, porque al punto se me van los ojos tras de mis ojos, tras su retrato, y desde que miro a mi mirada me siento vaciarme de mí mismo, perder mi historia, mi leyenda, mi novela, volver a la inconciencia, al pasado, a la nada.
> (pp. 864-5)

It seems reasonable to assume that Manuel's reactions to the lake are taken from Unamuno's own feelings about mirror-like surfaces. In this respect it seems that author and character are very similar.

Very soon Manuel is in visible decline, overwhelmed by the burden of his secret (p. 57). Lázaro tries to revive his flagging spirits with plans for a Catholic agrarian syndicate, but the priest dismisses this scheme as irrelevant to the business of religion, repeating Christ's words that 'My kingdom is not of this world' (p. 57). In the next chapter the hour of his death arrives. To Angela and Lázaro, Manuel compares himself to Moses who, having seen the face of God, must die. He enjoins upon brother and sister that they should prevent the parishioners from ever looking on the face of God. The experience of God (a concept in which Manuel seems to believe: see Chapter 4) appears to be, in Manuel's description, a personal confrontation with the absurdity of existence without him. This paradoxical 'death of God' theology is reinforced by Angela's suggestion that God may have deliberately caused Manuel's and Lázaro's sufferings as part of a mysterious plan (p. 77). He dies in the church, surrounded by the faithful, and the event causes such an impression that the simple Blasillo expires on the spot. Among the dead priest's belongings is found a breviary containing a dried carnation stuck to a piece of paper bearing a cross and a date. [6]

---

[6] P. 68. The significance of this discovery is obscure to me. Many critics hurry over it in silence. An exception is Shaw who claims that it symbolizes Manuel's loss of faith — 'hence the cross and the date' (*5*, p. 63). Even if Manuel had ever had much faith to lose, it is

A cult soon grows up around his grave, and the walnut cross, fashioned by Manuel himself, is supposed to have curative properties. Lázaro and Angela cannot believe in his death (see Chapter 5 for a consideration of the significance of this). Lázaro visibly pines for his old friend and stands for hours gazing into the lake which, associated as it is with Manuel's death wish and with the village supposedly drowned beneath the lake, is a powerful symbol for both characters of the nothingness beyond the grave. At the chapter's end he dies, himself virtually a saint (p. 74).

Angela lives on for many years in the village, and finally consigns the strange story to writing, hoping paradoxically that it will never be seen by the Church authorities. So the manuscript comes into Unamuno's hands, and he publishes it with (for Unamuno) surprisingly little additional comment of his own.

This, reduced to essentials, is the human story or plot of the novel, and on this level it requires little comment. It examines a dilemma which has no doubt exercised many men of the cloth: should one silence one's doubts and act out a Christian role before one's parishioners? Manuel chooses this path because he believes that to confess unbelief in an afterlife will destroy their contentment. From a strictly orthodox position, he thus puts himself in a state of mortal sin by administering the sacraments and taking confession when he is himself without real faith. But as I shall suggest later, Unamuno does not really help us to make up our minds whether he is right to act thus. Unamuno sidesteps the moral issue of Manuel's insincerity by saying that his parishioners would never have believed him anyway if he had confessed his unbelief, and one might also add that since large numbers of people (including the unconverted Lázaro) manage to live cheerfully without belief in an afterlife, Manuel's fears could be called ungrounded.

unlikely that he would commemorate the event. Perhaps the carnation refers in some oblique way to the Crucifixion; but, to anticipate the argument of Chapter 6, mysteries of this kind may be essential to the aesthetic effect of the novel.

But these questions should not be raised prematurely, and there is much more to be said about the novel before we can usefully consider them. It is important not to confine one's reading to the human interest element in a novel like this, because to do so will paradoxically blind one to its real human interest. In the preface to the 1933 edition Unamuno said that not only are the setting, clothes and physical appearance of the characters of no great importance in a novel, 'sino que tampoco importa mucho lo que suele llamarse el argumento de ella'. If we ignore this remark and read the text as a document about actual human relationships in a more or less contemporary setting, we must surely conclude that it is rather deficient. It portrays a plausible enough dilemma, but it merely sketches it. Several decades in Manuel's life are raced over in a bare twenty or thirty pages. The only explanation of his emotions we ever hear from Manuel is 'así me ha hecho Dios' (p. 27). Nor do we discover much about the personality of anyone in the novel: their appearances, mannerisms, speech and relationships are either suppressed entirely or merely hinted at; Manuel himself is, to a large extent, a blurred memory of someone else's account of his confessions. The setting is ethereal and unreal — a village by a lake and a mountain, located in some indeterminate place and time, and the whole drama is concluded in the bare space taken up by a couple of chapters in a normal novel.

It is almost as if Unamuno were deliberately trying to suppress certain information which would enable us to make up our mind about the events portrayed. The novel is full of tantalizing questions. Why did Manuel confess his unbelief to Lázaro? What was the date in his breviary? Why did Lázaro change so suddenly? Does Manuel believe in God? Did he act rightly or wrongly in deceiving his parishioners? Did the events happen as told or is Angela embroidering them? I suggest that Unamuno deliberately intended us to be puzzled by such questions. If the novel were merely an example of psychological realism it would be a rather unsubstantial contribution to the genre, lacking the detail necessary for producing the effect of rich and complex characters. I hope to show that we must look beneath the surface of the novel; that its very ambiguity and vagueness are deliberate devices designed to alert us to a more far-reaching message than could ever be carried at the level of mere psychological realism. The text is meant to be allusive, vague, impressionistic and uncertain so that we allow it to work on our imagination.

2.   The context of 'San Manuel Bueno, mártir'

WHEN trying to prove that a work is realistic, criticism usually indicates the connections between the text and the real life of the author and his world; so logically one ought to indicate the absence of these connections when one is trying to show that a text is non-realist. On the face of it, it is incongruous to open a discussion of *San Manuel Bueno, mártir* with an account of the period in which it was written, for it is not in any obvious way a comment on actual political or social events. But this is the point: the absence of links between the novel and the known world of history is an essential part of its nature, and we have to study the literary devices whereby this apparent independence of the text from contemporary life is achieved. This will reveal the extent to which the novel is a work of fiction in the strict sense of the word.

As soon as we consider the relationship between the novel and the life of its author and of Spain in the period when it was written, we are struck by the essential oddness of the text. It is simply not what we would expect either of the man or of the period.

San Manuel Bueno, mártir breathes an atmosphere of contemplative tranquillity and piety; it reads like the work of a man who has practised a lifelong contempt for politics. But it was in fact written during one of the most hectic years of Unamuno's public life, and at a time of intense political excitement in Spain — the year of the fall of the dictatorship of Primo de Rivera and of the unrest which led to the exile of King Alfonso XIII and the founding, in April of the following

year (1931), of the Second Republic. Nor did Unamuno stand
aloof from these events. It is absolutely wrong to allow works
like *San Manuel Bueno, mártir* to perpetuate the notion that
he was an unworldly man who confined his thoughts to eternal
spiritual questions. On the contrary, he was a highly political
animal, and no more so than at this time when he was at the
peak of a reputation for being a radical, even revolutionary,
progressive and republican. In fact he was publicly identified
as the chief symbol of the ascendant Republican movement
which was now in a feverish state, and his mere appearance
in 1930 could trigger anti-monarchist disorders. His progressive credentials at this time were internationally acknowledged.

This public reputation is an essential part of the
background of experiences and feelings which led him to
write *San Manuel Bueno, mártir*. It is necessary, however, to
grasp how much he had been personally hurt by his own
political involvements: to understand the extent to which he
came to feel that he had sacrificed his own happiness and even
spiritual integrity in the service of politics. It is the split
between public reputation and private misgivings which is,
after all, one of the central themes of the novel.

The event which had earned him acclaim as a radical hero
was his opposition to the dictatorship of Primo de Rivera. Six
years before, in February 1924, he had been sacked as Rector
of Salamanca University and professor of Greek and banished,
by order of the Dictator, to the not disagreeable place of exile
of Fuerteventura in the Canary Islands. In July the Dictator
relented, but Unamuno chose to go to Paris and announced
that he would not set foot on Spanish soil until Primo de
Rivera fell.

This quixotic gesture cost Unamuno bitter emotional suffering. Apart from his well-known dislike of France, he was a
man who needed the support of his wife and large family.
Life in Paris caused him to suffer a mental breakdown in
1925 whose effects lingered until after 1930. This experience
prompted him to write *Cómo se hace una novela,* a strange
and hysterical compound of reflections about death and violent
diatribes against the Dictator and Alfonso XIII which aptly
expresses the rather schizophrenic nature of Unamuno's im-

fear of death

mediate concerns in these years. The chief symptom of the breakdown was a recrudescence of Unamuno's thanatophobia, that morbid fear of death and nothingness that had never totally left him since March 1897, when he had suffered a similar collapse. [1] Of the 1925 crisis Emilio Salcedo notes that 'En aquellos días de París va don Miguel por las calles temiendo no llegar de un árbol a otro, con el corazón desbocado como un potro salvaje. De noche se despierta a veces sintiendo una fuerte punzada ... Junto al viejo fantasma de la idea del suicidio, como única liberación de su angustia solitaria, surge otro fantasma antiguo: el de la locura' (*4*, p. 283). The source of Salcedo's description seems to be the text of *Cómo se hace una novela* itself, a fictional work which may not necessarily reflect Unamuno's true condition. But the novel is transparently autobiographical, so we may assume that the condition of its protagonist, Jugo de la Raza, suicidal, hypochondriac, obsessed with death and earnestly seeking consolation in prayer and the New Testament, is probably true to life. Unamuno's fear of angina pectoris now had more substance than in 1897: he was sixty-one years old in 1925.

In August of the same year he fled Paris for Hendaye on the Franco-Spanish frontier, and his spirits were somewhat restored in these familiar Basque surroundings. He stayed there for the next four and a half years, his loneliness relieved by frequent visits from wife, family and friends; his hours of enforced leisure distracted by walks through the hills on the French side of the border. These were not very fertile years from a literary point of view: a few plays and the beginnings of a sort of poetic diary later entitled the *Cancionero*. But his political fury had not abated, and he spent much energy in writing invective against Alfonso and Primo de Rivera and was in active contact with such ardent Republicans as Blasco Ibáñez and Eduardo Ortega y Gasset. It is important, in order to appreciate the paradoxes of *San Manuel Bueno, mártir,* to note just how extreme his political attitudes could be at this time: when, in November 1925, violent attempts were made

[1] The parallels between the two crises are explored at excessive length by Zubizarreta, *15*.

to overthrow Primo de Rivera, leading to arrests and execu-
tions and the detention in Irún of armed gangs carrying in-
flammatory propaganda signed by Unamuno, he appears to
have advocated open violence: 'Por nuestra parte, considera-
mos legítimo cuanto se haga para derrocar una dictadura que
nos envilece y degrada ante el mundo' (quoted in *4*, p. 288).

In early 1928 we find that his private anxieties and depression have returned, and his decline was visible to his
friends who expressed concern about his health. In 1929 he
was once again worrying about angina and in the *Cancionero*
we see examples of that underlying longing for oblivion which
is perhaps the root of all his anxieties about death. Yet this
private melancholy seems to have robbed him of none of his
combativeness for in March 1929 he wrote a pamphlet accus-
ing the parents of Spain of cowardice for not following their
student children onto the streets to demonstrate against the
regime (*4*, p. 311).

In this labile state of mind Unamuno entered the year of
the composition of *San Manuel Bueno, mártir,* celebrated as
a symbol of democratic opposition to the dictatorship and
privately still prey to the phobias about death which had
afflicted him for most of his adult life. The gap could hardly
have been wider between the 'historical' Unamuno, the fiery
pamphleteer and orator, and the 'intrahistorical' Unamuno for
whom politics and history were irrelevant in the face of the
eternal problem of personal survival after death. He was now
plunged into a whirlwind of freely chosen and self-imposed
political activity which was to elate and exhaust him at the
same time.

On 26 January the tired and alcoholic Dictator resigned
and the King appointed an interim government pending general
elections. Honour satisfied, Unamuno now felt able to re-cross
the frontier, which he did on 9 February, walking across the
Hendaye-Irún bridge to a clamorous welcome. Two days later
he was in Bilbao being cheered by republican agitators. His
arrival in Salamanca was the signal for anti-monarchist distur-
bances and violence against the Rector of the University. Primo
de Rivera's death in Paris on 17 March inflamed republican

Unamuno also anti-king

feeling even more, and Unamuno's appearance in Madrid on 2 May was again the occasion of rowdiness, cries of '¡Muera el Rey!' and speeches against Alfonso by Unamuno. Unamuno was courteously but firmly accompanied out of Madrid by the police.

It was virtually in the midst of these stirring events that Unamuno visited the lake at Sanabria (1 June). Although he continued to be active throughout the year, particularly involved in campaigns for his re-election as Rector of Salamanca University, there is some indication that he suffered a crisis of despair or exhaustion at about the time he wrote the novel; a crisis which deepened in subsequent months and eventually destroyed his radical political enthusiasms. Unamuno was to prove a fair-weather friend of the Republic, and attentive readers could have spotted the warning signs of impending disillusion in the preface to the 1930 Spanish edition of *La agonía del cristianismo*. [2] This says that his political activities reflect little personal conviction, and are as much intended to persuade him of the usefulness of progress as they are designed to persuade his audiences. This is an important clue to the state of mind underlying *San Manuel Bueno, mártir:*

> En febrero de este año 1930, creí poder volver a mi España, y me volví a ella. Y me volví para reanudar aquí, en el seno de la patria, mis campañas civiles, o si se quiere, políticas. Y mientras me he zahondado en ellas he sentido que me subían mis antiguas, o mejor dicho mis eternas congojas religiosas, y en el ardor de mis pregones políticos me susurraba la voz aquella que dice: 'Y después de esto, ¿para qué todo?, ¿para qué?' Y para aquietar a esa voz o a quien me la da, seguía perorando a los creyentes en el progreso y en la civilidad y en la justicia, y para convencerme a mí mismo de sus excelencias. [3]

[2] First published in French in 1925. The Spanish introduction is dated October, a month before he wrote *San Manuel Bueno, mártir*.

[3] First Austral edition (Buenos Aires, 1942), p. 11.

Later in the same prologue he rejects the charge of pessimism,
arguing that much has been done in the field of both politics
and religion by people who really believe in neither:

> y sé todo lo que la religión y la política deben a los que
> han buscado consuelo a la lucha en la lucha misma, y
> aun sin esperanza y hasta contra esperanza de victoria.

One important conclusion to be drawn from such remarks is
that one can hardly blame the subsequent disastrous course
of the Second Republic for Unamuno's disillusion with the
progressive cause after 1931. Even before the Republic was
declared and things took a nasty turn with street fights and
desecration of churches, Unamuno was already in half a mind
to abandon politics for private religious reasons. He was not
a steadfast or reliable political ally, and was constantly prone
to desert causes at critical moments. The basic reason for this
seems to have been the periodic moods of self-revulsion which
came upon him in the very heat of his political enthusiasms.
He had deserted the Socialist Party in 1897, almost without
warning, [4] and in *Vida de Don Quijote y Sancho* (part I,
chapter 58) we read of a mood of violent self-hatred which
overcame him after giving a widely applauded public speech:
he says that on such occasions he goes home feeling like a
buffoon, a performer who has presented a false image of
himself. The problem was that Unamuno loved public acclaim
and celebrity and could never forego the temptations of seeking
notoriety; but he detested himself for succumbing and often
tried to rescue his self-esteem by writing books (like *San
Manuel Bueno, mártir*) which are contemptuous of the public
world and all its works.

The defeatist mood in the preface of *La agonía del cristianismo* did not however signal the immediate end of Una-

---

[4] Cf. 'Poco a poco' in *La Lucha de Clases,* 27 March 1897: 'momentos hay en que nos invade un sentimiento doliente, moviéndonos
a dejar la pluma y no persistir en la propaganda de estos artículos que,
en momentos tales, se nos antoja estéril o poco menos.' This apostasy,
as it was dubbed by the radical press, caused a great sensation.

muno's political enthusiasms. He expressed himself in even more radical terms when the Republic was finally declared, and he actually stood for and was elected as a Republican candidate to the Cortes. It was widely reported, in fact, that Unamuno expected to be invited to be President. 'Soy uno de los que más han contribuido a traer al pueblo español la República' he was to write of himself in the following year, [5] and anyone who imagines that Valverde de Lucerna represents Unamuno's ideal of a typical Salamancan or Zamoran village should recall that in April 1931 he declared himself especially satisfied at the size of the left-wing vote in Salamanca: this, he said, would dispel the notion that Salamanca was 'priest-ridden' *(levítica)*. [6]

Nevertheless, it is clear from *La agonía del cristianismo* that at about the same time as he wrote *San Manuel Bueno, mártir* he was musing about the part played in religious life by those who have no personal faith. No doubt this question inspired the novel he was to write the following month.

None of Unamuno's public political commitments is positively reflected in the novel, but we must bear them in mind in order to understand the text. With Unamuno it is especially important to remember that his works are rarely a direct expression of his own personality. Not that Unamuno liked to disguise himself in his writing: on the contrary, he always attempted to be true to himself. The problem was that when he set out to express himself he could not find a single, coherent self to express. If we do not take into consideration the things that Unamuno stood for in 1930, we shall fall into the trap of assuming the novel to be autobiographical and to be a straightforward reflection of the author's idea of reality. In some ways, however, it can be read as an attack on Unamuno's public beliefs and activities in the period 1923-30.

[5] 'La antorcha del ideal', *El Sol,* 23 June 1931.
[6] Quoted in González Martín, *10,* p. 73. On the contentious issue of divorce, for example, Unamuno was at this time declaring himself to be indifferent. See *10,* pp. 85-7.

3. *'San Manuel Bueno, mártir' as fiction*

THE foregoing brief account of the circumstances of Unamuno's life around the time when he wrote the novel was intended to introduce two statements about the text of the novel, one already made — that it apparently contradicts everything its author publicly stood for in 1930 — and the other now to be added: by its very structure and language, the novel is designed *not* to reflect or be connected with contemporary history or social conditions or (at least directly) with its author's own stated beliefs. In short, it is a highly fictionalized, mythical work with a strong element of mystery, unreality and even fantasy, and it achieves these qualities by a series of techniques whose aim may be said to be the systematic concealment of the text's own mode of production, i.e. a deliberate attempt by the author to disguise or obscure the events or emotions on which he has based his work. It is very much an anti-realist novel, a statement of which Unamuno would certainly have approved, and it is also a typically modern work of art in the sense that we cannot be sure to what the work refers: it is, in a complex and difficult sense, a work which is curiously enigmatic in its structure.

To take the first point, the novel seems to advocate a political line which is completely opposed to the progressive cause. This peculiarity in the novel was noted long ago by Arturo Barea, an ardent anti-fascist and one-time Communist. He remarked with some puzzlement that 'the first great work he wrote on his return to Spain could be taken, and often was taken, as his final rejection of all social changes that could lead to the destruction of the people's unquestioning traditional faith' (*6*, p. 54). Basdekis has more recently made a comment which must have been a common reaction from readers in

1931: '*San Manuel Bueno, mártir* does contain a rather distinct sociopolitical message, although it is not what might have been expected, given Unamuno's fierce opposition to dictatorship and monarchy' (*19*, p. 78).

The surprise of these critics is understandable. Manuel is offered to us as a fine example of wisdom and humanity, but he is utterly contemptuous about the social question and about enlightened politics in general. Lázaro, whose spiritual death is associated with radical progressivism, at first finds Manuel's hold over Valverde de Lucerna to be 'un ejemplo de la oscura teocracia en que él suponía hundida a España. Y empezó a borbotar sin descanso todos los viejos lugares comunes anti-clericales y hasta antirreligiosos y progresistas que había traído del Nuevo Mundo' (p. 36).

Lázaro scornfully dismisses priests who manage women and men, and the countryside of Spain which he describes as feudal and medieval. When Lázaro tries to interest Manuel in plans for the agrarian syndicate, the priest rejects such notions as relapses into his former progressivism. Religion, he continues, is not concerned with this world:

> ¿Cuestión social? Deja eso, eso no nos concierne. Que traen una nueva sociedad en que no haya ni ricos ni pobres, en que esté justamente repartida la riqueza, en que todo sea de todos, ¿y qué? (p. 58)

And he continues with the cynical, world-weary (but not aggressively reactionary) remark that Marx's dismissal of religion as the opium of the people precisely expresses religion's advantages: 'opio... Opio, sí. Démosle opio, y que duerma y que sueñe... Que jueguen al sindicato si eso les contenta' (p. 58). The phrase 'si eso les contenta' was added in the 1931 edition, and may have been designed to block our dismissal of Manuel as an obstructive conservative.

But by presenting Manuel as the hero, the novel apparently endorses his vision of rural contentment based on traditional values; and by associating Lázaro's 'resurrection' with his abandonment of anti-clerical radicalism, it associates the latter with spiritual death. Nowhere is the progressive political viewpoint treated favourably.

The novel does not only openly contradict its author's professed beliefs; in many ways it stands in a relationship of opposition to reality itself. It is deliberately fictitious, which is not to criticize it so much as to stress its essentially poetic, literary, as opposed to documentary, nature.

The novel does not present a lifelike picture of Spain in 1930, and Unamuno was well aware of this. In an article which appeared at about the same time as the first edition of the novel, he offered a version of rural life which is quite unlike the picture of bucolic calm prevailing in Valverde de Lucerna:

> En estos años se ha ido haciendo la educación civil y social del pueblo. Es ya una leyenda lo del analfabetismo. El progreso de la ilustración popular es evidente. Y en una gran parte del pueblo esa educación se ha hecho de propio impulso, para adquirir conciencia de sus derechos. España es acaso uno de los países en que hay más autodidactos. Hoy, en los campos de Andalucía y de Extremadura, en los descansos de la siega y de otras faenas agrícolas, los campesinos no se reúnen ya para beber, sino para oír la lectura, que hace uno de ellos, de relatos e informes de lo que ocurre en Rusia. [1]

We have seen that Unamuno was at pains in the prologue to prevent the reader identifying Valverde de Lucerna with any of the real villages at the lake. We are not really told where it is, or even when the events took place. Some critics attach a good deal of importance to the setting of the novel, [2] but Unamuno certainly did not. In his prologue he dismisses the setting as a major theme in this or any of his novels:

U didn't attach much import to the setting.

> tratando de narrar la oscura y dolorosa congoja cotidiana que atormenta al espíritu de la carne y al espíritu del

[1] 'La promesa de España', II, *El Sol*, 14 May 1931, reprinted in González Martín, *10*, pp. 77-81.

[2] Especially Turner, *21*, p. 125, and Marías, *11*, p. 114.

> hueso de hombres y mujeres de carne y hueso espirituales, ¿iba a entretenerme en la tan hacedera tarea de describir revestimientos pasajeros y de puro viso? (*OC*, II, p. 1184)

and he goes on to invoke Thucydides who aimed at writing ' "una cosa para siempre" ... ¡Para siempre!' The historical period of the novel, although we infer it to be at some point between about 1825 and 1930 since the text alludes to America and to contemporary events, is not important and is not emphasized by the author.

In fact every device is used to prevent us from making connections between this dreamlike, unreal setting and the realities of rural Spain. For a start Unamuno sets his story in a place of legend — Valverde de Lucerna is a fantastic village allegedly drowned beneath the lake, and it is not connected with Riba de Lago, Galande or any of the other villages of Sanabria. Moreover Unamuno puts this village in the imaginary diocese of Renada or 'Re-nada' — 'absolutely nothing' or 'Nowhere'. Valverde de Lucerna is also exempt from the historical factors conditioning the real life of Spain. It enjoys a tranquillity hard to imagine in the modern period: 'jamás en sus sermones se ponía a declamar contra impíos, masones, liberales o herejes. ¿Para qué, si no los había en la aldea?' (p. 18). By its name, origins and location, Valverde de Lucerna is a place literally out of this world.

We should be alerted not only by this unreal setting, but also by the transparently symbolic identity and function of the characters, to the mythical, symbolic nature of the text. The characters are in fact allegorical figures bearing a philosophical or religious message.

This is obviously true of Manuel Bueno, despite the fact that the idea of a sceptical priest may well have come to Unamuno from a real-life example. [3] He is pretty clearly

---

[3] In *Sensaciones de Bilbao,* in a sketch called 'Francisco de Iturri-barría', *OC*, X, pp. 635-9, Unamuno recalls an old priest he once knew who bore a melancholy secret similar to Manuel's. Unamuno told J. Brouwer in September 1936 that Manuel was 'un tipo sacado

Emmanuel, the Messiah, and I shall return to this in Chapter 4. Lázaro too is not really the provincial son made good in America, but the biblical Lazarus raised by Jesus from the dead; again, more of this later. Angela Carballino bears the Greek name *aggelē,* 'angel' or 'messenger', for it is she who brings tidings of this miracle of piety — even if she is a curious and unreliable story-teller. Blasillo symbolizes ordinary man, too weak and naive to be able to live with the burden of truth. Towards the end of his life Unamuno came more and more to have a low opinion of the potential of most men for independent thought, and Blasillo probably expresses his estimate of the emotional and intellectual scope of most mortals. Sánchez Barbudo goes so far as to suggest the name Blasillo really comes from Blaise Pascal whose *Pensées* (no. 418) advocate the suppression of reason and the adoption of mechanical habits of Church-going, prayer and so on as a sure road to faith (*14,* pp. 159-60). The parallel does not seem very convincing, but it may conceivably indicate the literary, symbolic origin of Blasillo.

This question of the mythical origins of the characters leads us, however, to consider another, much more important defamiliarizing, fictionalizing device in the novel. This is the time-honoured ruse of using an apocryphal narrator, in this case Angela. The version we have is an almost faithful copy of her original, 'sin más que corregir pocas, muy pocas particularidades de redacción' (p. 80).

The function of such imaginary story-tellers is always to distance the author from the subject-matter of the story, but the device assumes peculiar importance in this novel: Angela's personality and beliefs intervene in the story in numerous and subtle ways, and the extent to which the whole version of Manuel's life is mediated via her personality must be a crucial factor in any argument about the status of this novel as a more or less unequivocal record of Unamuno's beliefs.

To consider the question of narrative structure first, it is important to remember that the whole text is of the nature of

de la vida', and Salinas told Sánchez Barbudo that he had heard the same from Unamuno: Sánchez Barbudo, *14,* p. 151.

a second, even third-hand report of the life and feelings of
Manuel Bueno. Angela is never the direct recipient of Manuel's confessions — he does not really confide in her. Although
she intuits some mysterious sadness in the priest, she is astonished and disconcerted to hear from Lázaro that his piety is
merely an act: 'pero ¿es posible? exclamé, consternada' (p. 45).
Her response is to pray for him, but when she asks him,
shortly after, whether he believes, he is embarrassed and
dismisses her question with the answer '¡dejemos eso!' (p. 50).
All that she subsequently learns about Manuel's true feelings
comes not from him, but from Lázaro's reports. Moreover, she
is not really part of their conspiracy of humanitarian deceit.
Although, towards the end of her life, she wonders, briefly, if
she wholeheartedly believes (p. 77), she is, during the life of
Manuel, a firm believer. When Manuel asks her whether she
has the same faith as when she was ten, she replies affirma-
tively (p. 49). In this sense, Angela remains an outsider to the
events narrated: she is never really initiated into Manuel's
strange personal philosophy, and her reactions of surprise and
even shock are interposed, so to speak, between Manuel's life
and our possible response as readers. The effect of this is,
perhaps, to reassure the reader that there is another viewpoint
available in the novel; that the surprise and consternation of
Angela are perfectly valid reactions to the possibly dubious
example of the priest's campaign of deception.

But this is not the only way in which Unamuno distances
his account of the life of Manuel from a straightforward
chronicle. The crucial point — nearly always glossed over by
the critics — is that Angela's version of events is almost certainly unreliable, and that she herself is a fictitious character
who may also be fantasizing.

In the last two chapters, Unamuno does all he can to
confuse us about the truth of the story of Manuel Bueno. In
the last section or chapter, for example, he insinuates that
Angela is a fantastic character with a strangely autonomous
will:

> ¿Que se parece [este documento] a muchas otras cosas
> que he escrito? Esto nada prueba contra su objetividad,

> su originalidad. ¿Y sé yo, además, si no he creado fuera
> de mí seres reales y efectivos, de alma inmortal? ¿Sé yo
> si aquel Augusto Pérez, el de mi novela *Niebla,* no tenía
> razón al pretender ser más real, más objetivo que yo
> mismo, que pretendía haberlo inventado? (p. 80)

This bizarre theory that fictional characters are in some way
more real than the writers who invent them harks back to a
long-standing idea of Unamuno's that reality and fiction are
ultimately the same thing; that Don Quixote and Cervantes
are, from our point of view, equally existent since our only
knowledge of both is, after all, from books. This suggestive
idea is presumably included at the end of *San Manuel Bueno,
mártir* in order to remind us that the novel is a work of
imagination which, nevertheless, does not directly state the
author's own beliefs. Angela is, of course, an invention; but
she is none the less not merely a device inserted so that the
author can let us know his own thoughts through her. She is
in some way autonomous and her opinions are her own, just
as the other characters' are.

This is an important feature of the novel because it shows
once again just how difficult it is to get at the truth in this
work (not that it is ever particularly easy in any of Unamuno's
novels). As with an onion, we peel off layer upon layer of
fiction but at no point do we ever reach a core of certainty
on which we might base the statement: this is what really
happened; this is what the author really meant. Of course,
some readers might now despair and throw the work down as
pure fancy, a mystifying and pointless riddle; but as though
anxious to block this response of the impatient reader, Unamuno qualifies everything that has gone before with the remark
that though fictional, everything in the text is still in some
crucial sense true:

> De la realidad de este San Manuel Bueno, mártir, tal
> como me lo ha revelado su discípula e hija espiritual,
> Angela Carballino, de esta realidad no se me ocurre
> dudar; creo en ella más que creía el mismo santo; creo
> en ella más que creo en mi propia realidad. (pp. 80-1)

More confusions: despite its fictional nature, the story is to be taken very seriously: Manuel Bueno is in some sense more real than the author himself. Not real in a literal sense, but real in the sense of representing or incorporating an important truth. What this truth may be will be discussed later when we examine the allegorical message of the story.

Our familiar notions of truth and reality are further undermined by Unamuno's deliberate attempts to shake our confidence in Angela's reliability as a narrator. Initially it seems that her account of Manuel Bueno is accurate and true: 'De nuestro don Manuel me acuerdo como si fuese cosa de ayer, siendo yo niña, a mis diez años' (p. 8). But by the end of the novel we are disconcerted to find that she may have got it all wrong. She is now an old woman and her memory is failing: 'empiezan a blanquear con mi cabeza mis recuerdos' (p. 78). She goes on to tell us that, just as the contours of the landscape are blurred by the falling snow, so her recollection of the events recounted in the manuscript is growing dim:

> Está nevando, nevando sobre el lago, nevando sobre la montaña, nevando sobre las memorias de mi padre, el forastero; de mi madre, de mi hermano Lázaro, de mi pueblo, de mi San Manuel, y también sobre la memoria de mi pobre Blasillo... Y esta nieve borra esquinas y borra sombras, pues hasta de noche la nieve alumbra.
> (p. 78)

[margin annotation: Angela isn't sure if the events really happened]

As a result, she says, she is not at all sure whether the events really happened, or whether they are dreamed:

> Yo no sé lo que es verdad y lo que es mentira, ni lo que vi y lo que sólo soñé — o mejor dicho lo que soñé y lo que sólo vi—, ni lo que supe ni lo que creí. ... ¿Es que sé algo?, ¿es que creo algo? ¿Es que esto que estoy aquí contando ha pasado, ha pasado tal y como lo cuento? ¿Es que pueden pasar estas cosas? ¿Es que todo esto es más que un sueño soñado dentro de otro sueño?
> (pp. 78-9)

Thus another distortion occurs which increases the distance between the text and reality. We are left with the perplexing situation that *San Manuel Bueno, mártir,* far from being a documentary about real people and events, may be the fictions of an ailing fictional character — a dream within a dream.

There is another crucial way in which the novel is made fictional: its language. Hispanic studies have, during the last thirty years, been much influenced by the canons of realist criticism which prevailed in Spain as a reaction against the allegedly dehumanized literature of writers of the 1920s like Alberti, the early Lorca, Pérez de Ayala, Benjamín Jarnés and Francisco Ayala. There has consequently been a tendency to celebrate the best authors' language as close to ordinary colloquial Spanish: the great tradition of the Spanish novel, this argument runs, is represented by the Picaresque, Cervantes, Galdós, Alas and (in some versions) Baroja, and all these represent language supposed to be like the speech of ordinary people (though this is improbable enough).

The effect of such arguments is to make readers insensitive to the striking conventionalism and artificiality of much realist literary language. [4] If attention is not drawn to the highly literary, erudite quality of the language of *San Manuel Bueno, mártir* then it is indeed possible to fall into the naturalist trap of taking it for an everyday story of country folk. The text has none of the qualities of rural or unsophisticated language, and is not what one might expect from a country girl like Angela Carballino. It is highly ornate language; the work of a self-conscious stylist. Its grammar, word order and sentence structure are nothing like natural, spontaneous speech, even in the passages of dialogue. Unamuno makes no attempt, unlike Baroja and some other social realists, to imitate the *non*

[4] For the essentials of this argument I am indebted to Renée Balibar, *Les Français fictifs; le rapport des styles littéraires au français national* (Paris, 1974). Balibar insists on the basically fictitious, artificial language of much realist prose in France, and her point seems to me applicable, with modifications, to Castilian literature of the twentieth century with its complex interplay of official, Latinizing *Academia* syntax and vocabulary, and various levels of popular or regional usage. The striking archaism of Unamuno's language has often gone unnoticed.

sequiturs, dialectalisms and colloquialisms of everyday language. Consider the opening sentence of the novel:

> Ahora que el obispo de la diócesis de Renada, a la que pertenece esta mi querida aldea de Valverde de Lucerna, anda, a lo que se dice, promoviendo el proceso para la beatificación de nuestro don Manuel, o, mejor, San Manuel Bueno, que fue en ésta párroco, quiero dejar aquí consignado, a modo de confesión y sólo Dios sabe, que no yo, con qué destino, todo lo que sé y recuerdo de aquel varón matriarcal [5] que llenó toda la más entrañada vida de mi alma, que fue mi verdadero padre espiritual, el padre de mi espíritu, del mío, el de Angela Carballino. (p. 7)

Such language tells us what to expect in the rest of the novel. This 102-word sentence is complex and structured, and makes no concessions to rustic flavour such as we might expect if it were meant to mirror Angela's background and milieu. The elaborate ordering of sub-clauses and appositions displays all the qualities of a certain kind of recognisably literary Castilian. It is not an attempt to imitate the language of a woman who has spent only five years in a provincial convent and has never subsequently left her native village.

This point may be clarified by an examination of a few other passages:

> Cuando, al oficiar en misa mayor o solemne, entonaba el prefacio, estremecíase la iglesia, y todos los que le oían sentíanse conmovidos en sus entrañas. (p. 15)

> Don Manuel, tan blanco como la nieve de enero en la montaña, y temblando como tiembla el lago cuando le hostiga el cierzo, se le acercó con la sagrada forma en la mano ... (p. 43)

> Y cayeron temblando de sus pestañas a la yerba del suelo dos huideras lágrimas en que también, como en

---

[5] The Alianza text is corrupt here in reading 'patriarcal', thus losing the force of the paradox. Manuel combines male and female qualities in that he is both father and mother in one.

> rocío, se bañó temblorosa la lumbre de la luna llena.
> (p. 56; words supposedly spoken by Lázaro to his sister)

> Creeríase que el grito maternal había brotado de la boca
> entreabierta de aquella Dolorosa — el corazón traspasa-
> do por siete espadas — que había en una capilla del
> templo. (p. 16, added in the 1931 edition)

> Íbanse por las tardes de paseo, orilla del lago, o hacia
> las ruinas, vestidas de hiedra, de la vieja abadía de los
> cistercenses. (p. 41)

> Una noche de plenilunio — me contaba también mi her-
> mano — volvían a la aldea por la orilla del lago, a cuya
> sobrehaz rizaba entonces la brisa montañosa, y en el
> rizo cabrilleaban las razas de la luna llena ... (pp. 55-6,
> again words supposedly uttered by Lázaro. The Alianza
> edition reads *montañesa* for 'montañosa')

Such language is highly wrought and deliberately poetic. Forms
like *estremecíase, sentíanse, íbanse* mark it as archaic, formal
literary style, and words or phrases like *sobrehaz, cierzo, huide-
ras lágrimas* (normally *lágrimas huidizas*), *como en rocío* (for
the expected *como en el rocío*), *rizo, razas* (= *rayos*), the word
order of the sixth example, the contrived romantic, even
bathetic image of Manuel's tears bathed in moonlight, further
serve to set this language apart from that of ordinary speech
or even straight literary prose.

Even the dialogue bears little resemblance to ordinary
speech. It is not likely that Manuel or Lázaro would speak
dialect, but their utterances in this novel are often couched in
very bookish form:

> — Piensen los hombres y obren los hombres como pen-
> saren y como obraren, que se consuelen de haber nacido,
> que vivan lo más contentos que puedan en la ilusión
> de que todo esto tiene una finalidad. Yo no he venido a
> someter los pobres a los ricos, ni a predicar a éstos que
> se sometan a aquéllos. Resignación y caridad en todos
> y para todos ... (p. 58)

> — Aquí se remansa el río en lago, para luego, bajando a la meseta, precipitarse en cascadas, saltos y torrenteras, por las hoces y encañadas, junto a la ciudad, y así remansa la vida, aquí en la aldea. Pero la tentación del suicidio es mayor aquí junto al remanso que espeja la noche de estrellas, que no junto a las cascadas que dan miedo. (p. 53)

Or Lázaro's defence of Manuel to his sister:

> — Sí, fe, fe en el contento de la vida. El me curó de mi progresismo. Porque hay, Angela, dos clases de hombres peligrosos y nocivos: los que convencidos de la vida de ultratumba, de la resurrección de la carne, atormentan, como inquisidores que son, a los demás para que, despreciando esta vida como transitoria, se ganen la otra; y los que no creyendo más que en ésta ... (p. 70)

Future subjunctives (*pensaren, obraren*), the replacement of nouns by *éstos* and *aquéllos,* imagery like *remanso que espeja la noche de estrellas,* the use of sub-clauses interposed between verbs and their objects, e.g. *atormentan, como inquisidores que son, a los demás,* rhetorical vocatives separating subjects from their verbs — *hay, Angela, dos clases de hombres* — and the omission of *se* in *remansa la vida* are not features of Castilian as normally spoken. As in all Unamuno novels, the dialogue of *San Manuel Bueno, mártir* does not appear as an insertion of colloquial speech into a literary text, but essentially as a continuation of the text. The conversational language and the descriptive language are of the same elaborately literary style, nor are characters distinguishable by their speech. This is not the language of realism.

But then it should by now be clear that the novel is not a realist novel either, so there is no reason why Unamuno should have made concessions to natural language. If, for example, we read the text as naturalistic, how can we avoid dismissing Blasillo's death as low melodrama? The priest's most faithful disciple expires at exactly the same moment as he does. This unlikely coincidence, together with the heavily symbolic use of the lake as the watery tomb of a legendary

village, as the mirror of heaven and sea of death and also the
reflection of the vision of the void in Manuel's eyes, haunts
the novel as a powerful reminder of the text's essentially
poetic, mythical nature.

All this is in keeping with Unamuno's theories of the
novel. With the exception of *Paz en la guerra* (1896), one of
the last examples of the nineteenth-century realist tradition in
Spain, all his novels employ fictionalizing devices designed to
emancipate character and plot from specific spatial and chro-
nological contexts. We have seen how much emphasis he put
on this in the prologue to *San Manuel Bueno, mártir* where he
admits 'la desnudez de la parte material en mis relatos ...
dejándole al lector que la revista de su fantasía' (*OC,* II,
p. 1182). The setting is of no geographical importance and
local colour plays no part in the novel: Unamuno thought such
things merely distracting. [6] He took this theory as far away
from realism as he could, severing the language, physical appearance, period and location of his stories as much as he
could from the world around. A close reading of his novels
reveals how strange and unfamiliar their world ultimately is.

Unamuno himself is at pains to remind us at the end of
the novel that we have in our hands a work of fiction, not a
slice of life or a documentary. First he further distances himself
from the events portrayed by inserting his own dissenting point
of view about them, commenting that Manuel Bueno's dissim-
ulation was unnecessary since the simple villagers would never
have believed his merely verbal confession of unbelief. He then
stresses the literary, 'novelesque' nature of the text:

> este relato, si se quiere novelesco — y la novela es la más
> íntima historia, la más verdadera, por lo que no me ex-
> plico que haya quien se indigne de que se llame novela
> al Evangelio, lo que es elevarlo, en realidad, sobre un
> cronicón cualquiera ... (p. 82)

[6] For his quite immoderate attacks on what he thinks is the
superficiality of realist novels, see the preface to *Tres novelas ejemplares* (1920).

We are not to dismiss this work simply because it is fictitious: the fact that it is primarily a novel elevates it above mere documentary or 'cronicón'. But what are we to make of the remark that the New Testament is also a novel? The remark should alert us to the real purpose of *San Manuel Bueno, mártir:* its allegorical message. In fact one can grasp this allegorical nature of the text only if one puts out of one's mind the realist assumption that it is about real people in a real Spanish village. But before discussing this matter, I must give some account of Unamuno's own ideas about the nature of religious faith and its relationship to truth, and the way this subject is treated in the novel.

4. *Truth and myth in the novel and in Unamuno's thought*

THE central issue in the novel is the relative value of truth and myths: given the miserable facts of existence (specifically that we are doomed to die), which is preferable, happiness or knowledge? This question was probably the most fraught and sensitive of a whole range of problems which exercised Unamuno, and no account of *San Manuel Bueno, mártir* could be complete without some discussion of Unamuno's contradictory and passionate reflection on it.

There is obviously no doubt about Manuel's answer to the question. He commits himself to a life of deliberate falsehood because he believes that to confess his own doubts would plunge his simple and happy parishioners into the same despair that torments him. There are, he tells Lázaro, truths too awful to be told: 'la verdad ... es acaso algo terrible, algo intolerable; la gente sencilla no podría vivir con ella' (p. 46).

It is important here to remind oneself of two features of the novel which are constantly overlooked. The first has already been mentioned: Unamuno does not believe that Manuel's deception is necessary. On page 81 he remarks that if Manuel had confessed his doubts the ordinary villagers would never have believed him: 'habrían creído a sus obras y no a sus palabras ... Ni sabe el pueblo qué cosa es fe, ni acaso le importa mucho.' This disclaimer ought to (but rarely does) remind critics that Unamuno and Manuel are not the same person, because the former is openly insisting here that he would have acted differently under the circumstances. So much for crude biographical interpretations of the novel.

The second, even more neglected, point was raised at the beginning of the first chapter of this guide: nowhere does Manuel explicitly say he does not believe in God: he merely says that he cannot believe in the immortality of the soul. This is an important point because it shows that the novel is not actually atheistic, although several eminent *Unamunistas* have described it as such. [1] Angela records that when it came to reciting the Credo in unison, Manuel pronounced the opening words — 'I believe in God the Father' — in a loud and clear voice:

> Y no era un coro, sino una sola voz simple y unida, fundidas todas en una y haciendo como una montaña, cuya cumbre, perdida a las veces en nubes, era don Manuel. (pp. 17-18)

It is only when they come to the words 'I believe in the Resurrection of the Flesh and in Life everlasting' that Manuel's voice falters — 'y era que él se callaba' (p. 18). It is thus by no means clear that Manuel does not believe in God; merely that he does not believe in an afterlife. Since his sense of honesty prevents him from uttering the last words in the Credo (though it is not clear why he cannot pretend here, just as he does on every other occasion) we must assume that he is sincere when he speaks the opening words.

From a theological point of view this raises a vexatious problem. If he really does believe in God, Manuel's religious beliefs are, to say the least, peculiar; the question whether one can believe in God but reject the idea of immortality is best left to theologians, but it is certainly no common position. The only explanation that can be offered here is that Manuel's contradictory position reflects Unamuno's own conviction that the only crucial question for man is that of survival after death; the question of the existence or non-existence of God is a secondary problem. The point is, however, that we cannot assume that *San Manuel Bueno, mártir* is an account of an atheist position. Not only does the hero not deny the existence

[1] Particularly Sánchez Barbudo. See Chapter 5.

of God; the narrator Angela is, as was noted earlier, a pious
Catholic throughout Manuel's life — although she experiences
fleeting doubts in her old age. Moreover, she raises the possibility that the incredulity of Manuel and Lázaro might have
been part of God's incomprehensible design:

> Y es que creía y creo que Dios nuestro Señor, por no
> sé qué sagrados y no escudriñados designios, les hizo
> creerse incrédulos. (p. 77)

(One reason God might do this is to ensure that from time to
time a few men should face the misery of existence without
him, and thus preach religion with all the more passion and
conviction.)

To return to the question of the relative value of truth
and myth which is at the heart of this novel, Manuel's belief
that Catholicism makes people happy reflects one dimension
of Unamuno's own tormented enquiry into the value and
possibility of religious faith in the modern world. But his own
views on the matter were much less consistent than Manuel's.
In fact, he usually took the diametrically opposed position
that truth and suffering are far nobler than a contented life
of illusion.

It is instructive to trace the growth of Unamuno's own
attitudes towards Catholicism, which were of bewildering
complexity.

He could, when the occasion suited him (e.g. when de-
nouncing Primo de Rivera as a 'blasphemer') make fine pro-
fessions of Catholic piety:

> Yo, que fui educado por mi madre viuda en la más
> íntima y profunda piedad cristiana y católica; yo que
> he refrescado mis labios toda mi vida y a diario, para
> mantener en mi vida mi santa niñez con el Ave Ma-
> ría ...[2]

---

[2] *Dos artículos y dos discursos* (Madrid, 1930), p. 11; from a
vituperative article against Primo de Rivera dated January 1928.

And in fact he continued to act throughout his life very much like a Christian, even Catholic, believer. He always wore a crucifix, attended Mass frequently, insisted on saying the family rosary every day, regularly went into retreat in monasteries and read from the Gospels (in Greek) daily. He apparently only ever hit his son once, and this was for skipping Mass, and Francisco Maldonado, who once shared a hotel room with Unamuno, revealed that he could not sleep unless someone blessed him first. [3]

But all this is not to be taken at face value. In *Del sentimiento trágico de la vida* he says an adult can accept Catholicism only by denying his own intelligence, and when a conservative deputy actually ventured to praise Unamuno's 'espiritualidad y religiosidad' in a debate in the Cortes, Unamuno interrupted with a cry of '¡Yo no soy católico!' [4] In 1934, moreover, he made the very un-Catholic remark 'Yo creo que el mundo no tiene finalidad ... somos los hombres quienes le damos un sentido y una finalidad que no tiene'. [5]

These contradictions arose because Unamuno had always tended to look on religion in the same way as Manuel Bueno, as a consoling myth designed to hide the reality of existence from us. But unlike Manuel he never really made up his mind whether one ought or not to live by such comfortable myths.

Unamuno had been brought up in a pious atmosphere, but lost his faith in his late teens at Madrid University. He turned to it again, in 1897, as a result of a nervous breakdown whose primary symptom was a morbid fear of death. In fact he appears to have thought, in March of that year, that he had had a heart attack, and betook himself to the house of a priest in Alcalá de Henares where he spent the summer in spiritual exercises. [6] But we know from the Diary he wrote during these events that he never brought himself formally to re-enter the Church, an act which would have involved renunciation of his

[3] Details from Marrero, *12*, passim.

[4] Marrero, *12*, p. 60.

[5] 'Palabras recientes', *Ahora*, 25 December 1934.

[6] Details from Zubizarreta, *16*, and from letters to Unamuno in the Unamuno archives, Salamanca.

former beliefs, confession, absolution and re-admission to
Communion.

The Diary is a revealing account of a hopeless struggle
by an intelligent man to force himself to accept beliefs which
he knows are not true. At several points he prays for the
ability to believe what was patently false:

> Si llego a creer, ¿para qué más prueba de la verdad de
> la fe?

> Dame fe, Dios mío, que si logro fe en otra vida, es que
> la hay …

> ¿Por qué dudamos? ¿por qué no reconocemos a Jesús
> verdadero hijo de Dios? [7]

Unamuno never recovered the simple faith of his childhood,
and he in fact returned to his former way of life — although
the obsessive fear of death was never to leave him. The result
was a deep-seated tendency to envy Catholics for their supposed mental tranquillity, and to respect the Church as the
one institution that could offer a solution to the problem of
death — if one could only believe its teachings. The *Diario*
makes it clear that after 1897 Unamuno thought that the
choice before him was either Catholicism or a lifetime of
depression:

> Vivía dormido … alegre y animoso, sin pensar en la
> muerte más que como una proposición científica … He
> creído vivir feliz y me veo arrancado a esa felicidad.
> (p. 127)

> Voy a llevar una vida de interno pesar … (p. 106)

> Más de una vez me pongo a pensar *racionalmente* en
> mi estado; y acudo a todo lo de la herencia y el hábito
> de la niñez y el inconciente y mil otras razones, pero
> llega la hora y me siento impulsado a la iglesia y voy

[7] *Diario íntimo* (Madrid: Alianza, 1970), pp. 23, 26 & 212; this
passage was probably written in 1898.

*Unamuno was
totally obsessed
with a fear of
death.*

y oigo misa. Y sé que si esta razón vence volveré a las
angustias y congojas y ya no tendré paz en la vida.
(p. 141)

And we know that in his subsequent writings he frequently
expressed his bewildered inability to understand how anyone
could live at peace with the idea of his own extinction:

'Y ¿para qué quieres ser inmortal?' me preguntas. ¿Para
qué? No entiendo la pregunta, francamente, porque es
preguntar la razón de la razón, el fin del fin, el principio
del principio. [8]

What emerges from all this is an extremely complicated
attitude towards the Church and towards religious faith in
general.

In his most famous pronouncements, Unamuno adopted a
position which was the exact opposite of Manuel Bueno's. He
usually vigorously argued that men should face the truth about
existence at all costs, even of suffering. He was quite outspoken
about this, and poured scorn on the Manuel Buenos of the
world:

Hay espíritus menguados que sostienen ser mejor cerdo
satisfecho que no hombre desgraciado, y los hay también para endechar a la santa ignorancia. Pero quien
haya gustado la humanidad, la prefiere, aun en lo hondo
de la desgracia, a la natura del cerdo. Hay pues que
desosegar a los prójimos los espíritus ... Hay que inquie-
tar los espíritus y enfusar en ellos fuertes anhelos, aun
a sabiendas de que no han de alcanzar nunca lo anhe-
lado. Hay que sacar a Sancho de su casa ... ¿Qué es eso
de la santa ignorancia? La ignorancia, ni es ni puede ser
santa ... Si, sé la canción, sé lo de que 'buena almohada
es el Catecismo. Hijo mío, duerme y cree; por acá se
gana el cielo en la cama'. Raza cobarde. [9]

---

[8] *OC*, XVI, p. 175.
[9] *Vida de Don Quijote y Sancho, OC*, IV, pp. 227-8.

The point is also developed at considerable length in *Del sentimiento trágico de la vida,* which explicitly advocates destroying other people's religious convictions. In Chapter 11 he attacks the idea of letting people sleep or dream, and declares his aim to be to make them share his own suffering ('darles mi dolor') whether they want it or not:

> La caridad no es brezar y adormecer a nuestros hermanos en la inercia y la modorra de la materia, sino despertarlos en la zozobra del espíritu ... No hay que darse opio, sino poner vinagre y sal en la herida del alma. [10]

A passionate and uncompromising statement of this need for universal spiritual anguish is made in 'Verdad y vida' [11] which states that sincerity must be pursued whatever the cost: if all men told the naked truth, the world might threaten to become uninhabitable, but there would be eventual understanding; not only should we never lie, but we should actively preach hard and unpalatable facts; the believer who will not question his own beliefs lives in 'insinceridad y mentira'. This programme is also formulated as an implacable dogma in 'La correspondencia de un luchador':

primero la verdad que la paz.

> Ya conoces mi divisa: primero la verdad que la paz. Antes quiero la verdad que la paz ... Nada más triste que entercarse en vivir de ilusiones a conciencia de que lo son. Al que oigas decir 'Hay que mantener las ilusiones' estímale perdido — pues ¿cómo ha de mantenerlas si las sabe ilusorias? [12]

Even as late as 1931, after he had written *San Manuel Bueno, mártir,* we find him attacking the proverbially credulous faith of the charcoal burner: 'Salgamos de la ignorancia religiosa del carbonero.' [13]

[10] *OC,* XVI, p. 405.

[11] *OC,* IV, pp. 387-94; first published in 1908.

[12] *OC,* IV, pp. 395-401, at p. 395.

[13] 'Los milagros de la Virgen de Ezquioga', *El Sol,* 29 October 1931, quoted by Sánchez Barbudo, *14,* p. 153.

How is it possible that someone who wrote these uncompromising defences of truth at any price could also write a novel like *San Manuel Bueno, mártir* which makes a hero of a man who deliberately propagates a myth in order to stop people thinking for themselves?

The fact is that, in these appeals for uncompromising honesty, Unamuno was presenting as passionate convictions views which he only half-heartedly held. As early as 1898 he had put into print the exact opposite: that it is preferable for ordinary men not to think about the problems of existence. In a violent attack on progressive social modernization, he argued that the ignorance and backwardness of the Spanish *pueblo* are sure guarantees of their spiritual peace: the indifference of the common people towards all talk of social reform and modernization is proof of their 'cristiana salud'; the *pueblo* are not afraid of death, which terrifies only intellectuals; the peasant of El Toboso lives no less happily than the citizen of New York; far better the Middle Ages than the present, 'aquella hermosísima Edad Media, llena de consoladores ensueños'; progress merely stops us dying in peace; let the simple Sancho Panzas of this world live on 'en paz y en gracia de Dios en su atraso e ignorancia'. [14] These are strange words from someone who in the same year was studying Marx's *Capital* and had recently called himself 'más socialista que antes'. [15]

There is some evidence that this reactionary attitude, which sporadically surfaces in Unamuno's work, particularly in the travel articles and poems, became stronger after about 1932 when his disillusion with the Republic increased. An example is the article 'Almas sencillas', published in *Ahora* on 21 October 1933, at about the same time as the first book edition of *San Manuel Bueno, mártir* appeared. [16]

[14] 'La vida es sueño', *OC*, III, pp. 407-17.
[15] See J. W. Butt, 'Determinism and the Inadequacies of Unamuno's Radicalism, 1886-97', *Bulletin of Hispanic Studies*, XLVI (1969), 226-40, at p. 229.
[16] In *OC*, X, pp. 991-4.

This throws much light on the question of Unamuno's own attitude towards Manuel Bueno. It begins with a disclaimer: an author cannot be expected to know more about his characters than a reader. On the contrary, it is not the author who speaks through his characters, but the characters who speak through the author: 'Yo ... sigo sosteniendo ... que no es el autor de una novela ... quien mejor conoce las intimidades de ella y que son nuestras criaturas las que se nos imponen y nos crean.' Once again, we are warned not to identify Manuel Bueno with Unamuno.

He then addresses himself to the problem of whether he admires Manuel Bueno's attempts to deceive the common people. Apparently not:

> Ah, no; hay que despertar al durmiente que sueña el sueño que es la vida. Y no hay temor, si es alma sencilla, crédula, en la feliz minoría de edad mental, de que pierda el consuelo del engaño vital. Al final de mi susodicha historia digo que si don Manuel Bueno y su discípulo Lázaro hubiesen confesado al pueblo su estado de creencia — o mejor de no creencia —, el pueblo no les habría entendido ni creído, que no hay para un pueblo como el de Valverde de Lucerna más confesión que la conducta, 'ni sabe el pueblo qué cosa es fe ni acaso le importa mucho'. Y he de agregar algo más, que ya antes de ahora he dicho, y es que cuando por obra de caridad se le engaña a un pueblo, no importa que se le declare que se le está engañando, pues creerá en el engaño y no en la declaración. *Mundus vult decipi;* el mundo quiere ser engañado. Sin el engaño no viviría. ¿La vida misma no es acaso un engaño?

This seems to say, like the close of the novel, that it makes no difference whether you tell the truth or not: people will always prefer illusions. The question of whether Manuel did right or wrong does not arise: it would have been the same either way.

But a few lines later Unamuno seems to take a position more favourable to Manuel:

¡Si fuera posible una comunidad de sólo niños, de almas
sencillas, infantiles! ¿Felicidad! No, sino inconciencia.
Pero aquí en España, la inconciencia infantil del pueblo
acaba por producirle mayor estrago que le produciría la
íntima inquietud trágica. Quítesele su religión, su ensueño de limbo, esa religión que Lenin [sic] declaró que era
el opio del pueblo, y se entregará a otro opio, al opio
revolucionario de Lenin. Quítesele su fe — o lo que
sea — en otra vida ultraterrena, en un paraíso celestial,
y creerá en esta vida sueño, en un paraíso terrenal revolucionario en el comunismo o en cualquier otra ilusión
vital. Porque el pobre tiene que vivir. ¿Para qué? No le
obligues a que se pregunte en serio para qué, porque
entonces dejaría de vivir vida que merezca ser vivida.

This is extremely ambiguous at crucial points, but the last
lines come very close to saying that men must have some myth
to live by, and since all are false it really doesn't matter which
they believe; if they are already Catholics let them alone, for
they will only adopt other equally nonsensical ideas. This
would be in line with Manuel Bueno's philosophy in the sense
that it shows belief in anything to be preferable to knowledge
about the meaninglessness of life. And indeed, in another
article written about the same time, Unamuno says that one
ought to deceive men to make them happy: 'Todo el que se
proponga hacer la dicha — la emancipación — del pueblo, pro-
letario o no, tiene el deber de engañarle.' [17] Two years later
he also echoed Manuel in defining the function of religion to
be that of consoling us, not of improving us: 'No es cosa de
hacerle al hombre bueno o malo, sino de consolarle de haber
nacido.' [18]

It may be objected that all this is unhelpful: are we to
admire or to condemn Manuel for deceiving the people? But
it should by now be clear that we cannot appeal to Unamuno
to solve this dilemma for us. Indeed, by citing the epistle of

[17] 'Las ánimas del purgatorio', in *La ciudad de Henoc,* quoted by
Sánchez Barbudo, *14,* p. 157.
[18] 'Cartas al amigo XVI', *Ahora,* 21 October 1934, in *OC,* XI,
p. 1035.

St Jude on p. 81 (see next chapter for further discussion of this quotation) Unamuno is pretty clearly trying, among other things, to warn us against sitting in moral judgement on Manuel. Unamuno never adopted a wholly consistent position on the value of myths versus truth. Moreover his novels are not ethical documents in the sense that they explicitly evaluate their characters' actions. He said this several times himself when he disclaimed specific moral advocacy in his novels. In the preface to *Tres novelas ejemplares* he sharply distinguishes between novels which are morally exemplary in the sense of didactic, and those which are aesthetically exemplary: his novels are the latter, i.e. *exempla* in the sense of 'instances' or 'cases' of human conduct, not models or anti-models. He repeated the argument in 'Almas sencillas' where he notes the insuperable problem most readers have in separating moral and aesthetic judgements.

Unamuno had no final position on this vexed question of truth versus illusion. His novel merely dramatizes one of the horns of a dilemma on which he was caught for most of his life after 1897. We should not enquire whether Manuel's solution represents Unamuno's, for as he himself said,

> Una cosa es que todos mis personajes novelescos, que todos los agonistas que he creado, los haya sacado de mi alma, de mi realidad íntima... y otra cosa es que sean yo mismo. (*OC*, II, p. 975)

5. *The allegory*

Creo en [la realidad de este San Manuel Bue-
no]... más que creía el mismo santo... (p. 81)

IN Chapter 3 I argued that *San Manuel Bueno, mártir* is highly
fictional and contains a strong element of fantasy. We must
recall this point in order to appreciate fully the most extraor-
dinary and subversive feature of the novel: its allegorical
message.

For the novel is, in a sense, not about a Spanish village
and its sceptical human priest at all, but about Jesus Christ
himself. Its scandalous implication is not that Manuel Bueno
acted humanely in deceiving his flock into belief, but that
Jesus himself went to the Cross knowing full well that what
he had taught men was false. Jesus, the novel suggests, was a
sceptic who, out of pity for ordinary men, allowed himself to
suffer a martyr's fate so that they might believe. By deliberately
suffering a cruel death, Jesus gave men, who are as helpless
and simple as Blasillo, a myth, a *mentira vital,* with which to
console themselves.

The text of the novel is strewn with hints and clues as to
the real identity of Manuel Bueno, but critics have generally
given this aspect of the novel rather cursory attention. [1] The
vogue of existentialist or psychological interpretation in *Una-*

[1] The allusions to Jesus have often been noted, but no critic, to
my knowledge, ventures to argue that such parallels constitute the
essential message of *San Manuel Bueno, mártir.* Batchelor, *17,* pp. 101,
191, and Falconieri, *23,* pp. 128-41 are both sharply aware of the
presence of the biblical story in the novel, but neither reads it as
allegory.

munismo has generally distracted attention from the biblical
dimension of the story and focussed it on the contemporary
relevance of Manuel's dilemma. The result seems to me to be
a misreading.

The novel is structured quite closely on the New Testament, and it should be recalled that Unamuno carried a copy
wherever he went and read from it every day. Manuel is
clearly Jesus, as his name tells us, in Hebrew 'Immanuel', the
prophet Isaiah's name for what was later taken to be the
Messiah: 'Behold, a virgin shall conceive, and bear a son, and
shall call his name Immanuel' (Isaiah vii.14). As a result of
this name, Manuel's patron is Christ himself — 'su santo pa-
trono era el mismo Jesús Nuestro Señor' (p. 15).

Further allusions to the biblical identity of Manuel are best
raised in order of their appearance in the novel.

We are told early on that he had the ability to cure the
sick, and Unamuno calls him a 'healing pool', insinuating that
like Jesus he could wash away men's sins. It is impossible not
to recall Jesus's miracles on the shores of Galilee:

> En la noche de San Juan, la más breve del año, solían
> y suelen acudir a nuestro lago todas las pobres mujeru-
> cas, y no pocos hombrecillos que se creen poseídos,
> endemoniados, y que parece no son sino histéricos y a
> las veces epilépticos. Y don Manuel emprendió la tarea
> de hacer él de lago, de piscina probática y tratar de ali-
> viarles y si era posible de curarles. Y era tal la acción
> de su presencia, de sus miradas, y tal sobre todo la dul-
> císima autoridad de sus palabras y sobre todo de su voz
> — ¡qué milagro de voz! — que consiguió curaciones sor-
> prendentes. (p. 14)

On Good Fridays the sound of his 'voz divina' has a
tremendous effect on the congregation when he utters Jesus's
words, '¡Dios mío! ¡Dios mío! ¿Por qué me has abandonado?',
words which make the whole village tremble — just as the
earth trembled at the Crucifixion: 'y era como si oyesen a
Nuestro Señor Jesucristo mismo, como si la voz brotara de
aquel viejo crucifijo' (p. 16).

On one occasion Manuel's mother, on hearing these words, cries out '¡Hijo mío!'. Angela remarks that it was as if they had come from an image of the Virgin in a side chapel (p. 16).

When confronted by a judge from a neighbouring town who asks Manuel to discover the author of a crime, the latter repeats Christ's words, 'No juzguéis para no ser juzgados' (Matthew vii.1) and 'dé usted, señor juez, al César lo que es de César, que yo daré a Dios lo que es de Dios'. In the same chapter we are also told that Manuel had skills as a carpenter: he cuts six planks from the walnut tree and also makes toys for the children. Traditional stories tell of Jesus learning carpentry from his father.

Gazing into the lake Manuel longs to turn it into wine; and in Chapter 13 an obvious parallel between him and Jesus is drawn — the resurrection of Lazarus/Lázaro (John xl.1-45). Lázaro is symbolically raised from the spiritual death of progressive anti-clericalism: 'él me hizo un nuevo hombre, un verdadero Lázaro, un resucitado ... Me dio fe' (p. 70). Further proof of Manuel's identity as Jesus comes during Lázaro's Communion when the congregation, noticing how moved Manuel is, murmur '¡Cómo le quiere!', words taken from John xi.35-6: 'Jesus wept. Then said the Jews, Behold how he loved him!' At that point a cock crows, reminding us of the scriptures even if the allusion is not very clear. Perhaps the prophetic sound points to Lázaro's and Manuel's self-betrayal. Perhaps it is inserted merely to recall the biblical foundation of the story.

It is crucially important to note here that the first manuscript draft of the novel bore the epigraph 'Lloró Jesús', but no doubt because he felt that this quotation made Manuel's identity too transparent, Unamuno deleted it in the printed versions. Lázaro seems to know the real reason why he has taken Communion. When he is telling his sister about his act of pious sacrilege, he hears Blasillo go past crying 'My God, my God! Wherefore hast thou forsaken me?':

Y Lázaro se estremeció creyendo oír la voz de don Manuel, acaso la de Nuestro Señor Jesucristo. (p. 45)

It is during Manuel's last Easter that the most explicit
statement about Jesus's true fate is made. While Angela is
leaning forward to take the Sacrament, Manuel whispers in
her ear ' "Reza, hija mía, reza por nosotros." Y luego, algo
tan extraordinario que lo llevo en el corazón como el más
grande misterio, y fue que me dijo con voz que parecía de
otro mundo: "y reza también por Nuestro Señor Jesucristo ..." '
(p. 61). Obviously no Catholic prays for the soul of Christ,
for if God himself is not saved the religion makes no sense.
Angela is stunned by this revelation: 'me levanté sin fuerzas
y como sonámbula. Y todo en torno me pareció un sueño.'
She returns to her house, takes the crucifix and recalls the
tragic '¡Dios mío! ¡Dios mío! ¿por qué me has abandonado?'
of 'nuestros dos Cristos, el de esta Tierra y el de esta aldea'.
She has clearly understood the full meaning of Manuel's words
— that she must pray for Jesus's soul. But the matter is too
sensitive for further discussion, and when she raises it the
following day Manuel refuses to talk (p. 62).

On his death, the villagers rush to the house and divide
his clothes, like the Centurions (Matthew xxvii.35, Luke xxiii.
24). And even now a 'Resurrection' takes place, since Manuel's
faithful followers are unable to believe in his death and some
of them possibly actually see him again walking by the lake:

> Nadie en el pueblo quiso creer en la muerte de don Ma-
> nuel; todos esperaban verle a diario, y acaso le veían,
> pasar a lo largo del lago y espejado en él o teniendo por
> fondo la montaña; todos seguían oyendo su voz, y todos
> acudían a su sepultura, en torno a la cual surgió todo
> un culto. (p. 69)

In fact old women come to touch the walnut cross that he
made himself.

The idea that some leading light of the Church died
without believing in an afterlife is further implanted in our
minds by Lázaro's report of Manuel's words that more than
one of the great saints, perhaps the very greatest himself, had
died without believing in the afterlife (pp. 72-3). Exactly
whom Manuel means is not very clear. Given the rather

gnomic nature of many of the utterances in this book, and the
general air of mystery and allusiveness it contains, Manuel
may well have been referring to Jesus himself who would be,
after all, a saint for someone who thought of him as an ordinary mortal who performed pious, but essentially non-mirac-
ulous, deeds. However, in view of the epigraph to the novel,
he probably means St Paul. The quotation from I Corinthians
xv.19, 'Si sólo en esta vida esperamos en Cristo, somos los
más miserables de los hombres todos' comes in the context of
a discussion of the probability that Jesus rose from the dead.
Paul argues that the whole question of human immortality
hinges on the Resurrection, which he thus pushes to the centre
of the Christian message: 'For if the dead are not raised, it
follows that Christ was not raised' (xv.16). This, of course, is
the precise point of the novel — with its attendant implication
that if Christ was not raised, then nor are men. . . .

Unamuno himself concludes the novel with a mysterious
allusion:

> Y ahora antes de cerrar este epílogo, quiero recordarte,
> lector paciente, el versillo noveno de la Epístola del olvi-
> dado apóstol San Judas ... donde se nos dice cómo mi
> celestial patrono, San Miguel Arcángel ... disputó con
> el Diablo ... por el cuerpo de Moisés y no toleró que se
> lo llevase en juicio de maldición, sino que le dijo al
> Diablo: 'El Señor te reprenda.' Y el que quiera enten-
> der, que entienda.

What can these lines, 'el que quiera entender, que entienda'
mean? Unamuno is apparently letting us know that some important point is being made, but he chooses to quote one of
the most obscure epistles about which biblical scholars disagree.
Jude is apparently warning the faithful against some dangerous
or false beliefs in the new Christian religion. 'Certain persons
who have wormed their way in ... the enemies of religion'
(Jude 4); these heretics have dreams which 'lead them to defile
the body, to flout authority, and to insult celestial beings' (8-9):

> In contrast, when the archangel Michael was in debate
> with the devil, disputing the possession of Moses' body,

> he did not condemn him in insulting words [alternative
> translation 'charge him with blasphemy'] but said, 'May
> the Lord rebuke you!'

The scholarly Sánchez Barbudo takes this quotation as meaning
that Manuel Bueno does not really deserve reproach for
having deceived his parishioners, just as he (Unamuno) does
not deserve the reproach of his readers for deceiving them for
years into thinking he was a Christian. [2] It seems more likely
that this quotation is a reminder to us that, just as Michael
admonished the Devil not to judge Moses hastily and at the
same time abstained from passing judgement on the Devil
(who is a celestial being), so we too should refrain from passing
judgement on the 'celestial being' Manuel/Immanuel. It is not
for us to condemn such a saintly person, even for the sin of
deceiving men so as to make them happy. We cannot presume
to know what is the right course of action in face of the fact
of human weakness and misery.

It is difficult not to conclude from the obvious parallels
that Unamuno deliberately based his story on the New Testament; that he wishes to implant in our minds, in an oblique,
allusive way, the idea that Jesus willingly became the chief
martyr of a faith which he founded without really believing
in it himself, and that he did so that we might all live
contentedly like the parishioners of Valverde de Lucerna.
Unamuno is implying that Jesus was no more (or less) than a
human hero who suffered death in order to create and reinforce
human illusions.

Is it conceivable that Unamuno would build this contro-
versial claim into his novel? In fact there are clues elsewhere
in his works which suggest that he was inclined to believe that
Jesus did not believe in the immortality of the individual soul.

In at least two passages he argues that primitive Christianity was probably — or possibly — aneschatological, i.e.
unconcerned with the next world. In *Del sentimiento trágico
de la vida* he puts this idea forward rather tentatively when he

---

[2] *14*, p. 156.

suggests that the notion of the immortal soul is an idea alien
to Jesus whose doctrines were chiliastic:

> Hase afirmado del cristianismo primitivo, acaso con pre-
> cipitación, que fue claramente anescatológico, que en él
> no aparece claramente la fe en otra vida después de la
> muerte, sino en un próximo fin del mundo y estableci-
> miento del reino de Dios, en el llamado quiliasmo. [3]

Chiliasm or millenarianism denotes belief in an essentially
social or collective golden age to come in this world rather
than an individualist belief in a personal afterlife in some
other, non-material spiritual world. Unamuno goes on to quote
Jesus's remark to his disciples (Mark ix.1) that 'there are some
of those standing here who will not taste death before they
have seen the kingdom of God already come in power', a
statement which might conceivably be read as suggesting that
the dead are now really dead rather than lodged in spiritual
form in Heaven or Hell, an interpretation which leaves the
whole idea of the immortal soul in some doubt.

Among the Jews, Unamuno says, the idea of a personal
life after death was neither 'general ni clara' (ibid., p. 186).
In fact Unamuno says that the tragic sense of life, i.e. the
agonizing realization of human mortality, came to the Jews
only with the death of Jesus himself, 'la muerte del hombre
perfecto... la suprema revelación de la muerte, la del hombre
que no debió morir y murió' (ibid., p. 189). It was only after
Jesus's death that the distinctive Christian notion of personal
immortality emerged. This doctrinal step was taken by men
like Paul who did not know Jesus personally and invoked the
idea of the eternal personal soul in order to defend the (for
many of his contemporaries) absurd notion of the Resurrection,
and also to bolster the flagging morale of the Christians by
promising them an individual life in Heaven in place of or as
well as the immediate end of the world which Jesus had
promised and which showed no signs of arriving. This idea,
Unamuno says, was taken by Paul from Greek Platonic

[3] *OC,* XVI, p. 185.

philosophy, so it is abundantly clear that Unamuno was inclined to take the idea of the immortal soul to be a later addition to Christian belief not really justified by the scriptures.

This idea is more forcefully stated in *La agonía del cristianismo,* written some ten years after the above passage and not long before *San Manuel Bueno, mártir:*

> Jesús de Nazaret creía acaso en la resurrección de la carne, a la manera judaica, no en la inmortalidad del alma, a la platónica y en su segunda venida al mundo. Las pruebas de esto pueden verse en cualquier libro de exegesis honrado. (*OC,* XVI, p. 476)

In other words, there is no afterlife, but merely the chance of a better life here on earth. In the same work he neatly (and characteristically) sidesteps the issue of whether Jesus was really raised from the dead by attributing his resurrection to popular belief: 'pero luego que murió Jesús y renació el Cristo en las almas de sus creyentes ... nació la fe en la resurrección de la carne y con ella la fe en la inmortalidad del alma' (p. 477). Catholicism's future task was to make the ambiguous message of early Christianity, in itself unlikely to satisfy the ordinary man's desperate longing for faith in his own survival beyond the grave, into a rigid dogma which guaranteed that all men will live forever.

Unamuno was thus inclined to distinguish between what Jesus taught and what the Church subsequently preached, and this seems to indicate clearly enough that for Unamuno the figure of Jesus was much more human and potentially tragic than the divine being of later doctrine.

Half-concealed within Unamuno's work we can glimpse from quite early on the gradual growth of his admiration for a man like Jesus or Manuel who could sacrifice everything for the sake of an ideal of human happiness. After the crisis of 1897 (one should recall the entry in the *Diario:* '¿Por qué no reconocemos a Jesús verdadero hijo de Dios?') he concerned himself more and more with the problem of faith, specifically with the ways in which a man could manage to believe or even to make true by an act of will, things that he knows in

his heart are false. Unamuno fixed on Don Quixote as an
example of the tragic hero who, by an act of willpower, affirms
faith and life over the dismal facts of reason and common
sense. In *Vida de Don Quijote y Sancho* the mad knight is
offered as a model for an incredulous age because he has the
courage to affirm that which reasonable men deny: he ignores
the evidence that a helmet is really a basin. Nor did Unamuno
hesitate to draw veiled comparisons between Don Quixote and
Jesus himself, as for example when he calls him 'Nuestro
Señor Don Quijote' and his lady 'nuestra señora Dulcinea del
Toboso' to whom he commends himself in language which
directly parodies that of Catholic prayers (*OC,* IV, p. 178).
In the 1933 prologue to *San Manuel Bueno, mártir* the link
between Don Quixote, Manuel Bueno, and presumably Jesus,
is made when Unamuno calls the fates of both Manuel and
Don Quixote 'quijotescos los dos' (*OC,* II, p. 1193).

But the nearest Unamuno came to an unequivocal statement about the nature of Jesus — and this is, in general, a
matter about which he equivocated constantly — is in the poem
El Cristo de Velázquez, a series of meditations on the figure,
specifically the body, of the crucified Jesus. This is a poem
which has some magnificent passages, but it is exasperatingly
cryptic on the crucial question of whether Jesus was in fact
divine. The poem is full of intense admiration for his heroic
sacrifice which has made men live again — 'Eres el hombre
eterno/que nos haces hombres nuevos' (Part I, lines 1-10) —
and given a sense of purpose to human existence: 'con tu
muerte has dado/finalidad humana al Universo/y fuiste muerte
de la Muerte al fin' (III, lines 1-3). By Jesus's death men have
learnt to hope. But what the poem does not say is that he was
actually raised from the dead. Rather the poem celebrates
Jesus's example as a source of a consoling belief in resurrection
for men. The fourth part, entitled 'Muerte', says nothing of
his resurrection.

All this evidence suggests that it is not implausible to read
San Manuel Bueno, mártir as a veiled hint about the true
nature of Christianity. Unamuno believed that it — especially
the Catholic version — more than any other religion, has the

power to make men believe in their own survival, for it is guaranteed by the appalling death of the man who first preached it. Unamuno had a lifelong respect for Christianity's concern with human happiness and a deep envy for those who could believe its teachings. It is logical, therefore, that he should admire the man who founded it and set the seal of his own life on it. But it also seems that Unamuno suspected his teachings were a myth, designed to preserve our sanity in the face of a meaningless existence too horrible to contemplate in all its brevity and pointlessness.

6. *Symbols*

REFERENCE has been made in previous pages to the symbolism used in *San Manuel Bueno, mártir*, and the subject now calls for more detailed comment.

Most critics agree in emphasizing the importance of the ~~lake + mountain~~ symbols in the novel; most of them list what they take to be the major ones, but most also disagree about their meaning. To take the example of the lake and mountain alone, Turner asserts that they represent stability and permanence (*21*, p. 125); Pelayo Fernández claims they stand for the villagers' faith (because mountains point upwards) and eternity respectively (*24*, p. 127 and 137). Shaw suggests that they stand for God's heaven and the 'placid faith of the villagers' (*5*, p. 64); Gullón interprets the lake as standing for 'nothingness' (*20*, p. 337); and Falconieri takes it, among other things, for the villagers' tears (*23*).

The student may be forgiven for being discouraged by such a disconcerting variety of interpretations which have little in common save the fact that in no case do the critics explain why they assign a particular meaning to a particular symbol. In fact nowhere do we find a discussion of the criteria whereby we can decide what is a symbol and what is not: it is merely ~~guesswork~~ assumed that lake, wind, snow and mountain are symbolic, and their values are assigned by more or less inspired guesswork.

Is there any way we could finally decide about the meanings of symbols in *San Manuel Bueno, mártir* (or in any other modern literary work for that matter)? The answer must be negative: there can be no objective solution to the question, because symbolic values depend ultimately on their power to evoke associations in the reader's mind — and such associations cannot, by their nature, be predicted for individuals.

As a result, the remarks about symbols in *San Manuel Bueno, mártir* which follow will be tentative and cautious.

Two general points may appropriately introduce the discussion. The first is that any attempt to strive for too much specificity in the interpretation of symbols is doomed to fail, because symbols in a work like this do not stand for concrete, definable concepts so much as for clusters of emotions. In Chapter 3 of this guide a description was given of the devices whereby Unamuno generates an atmosphere of vagueness and uncertainty around the characters and events of the novel. The chief symbols in the novel, the lake, mountain, wind, snow and the goatherd singing on the mountain-side (p. 54), are likewise nowhere specifically defined or given fixed values. In fact they often appear accompanied by qualifications which emphasize the vagueness of the associations they arouse in the mind of the character who is contemplating them. The lake's healing powers may be a myth (p. 14), the village submerged beneath its waters is probably a fiction, the blue of the waters is associated with an enigma ('no sé qué honda tristeza', p. 32), snow falling on the lake and settling on the mountainside is a mystery ('¿has visto, Lázaro, misterio mayor ...?', p. 54); and at the end of the story snow is again associated with vagueness as it does to the contours of the landscape what the ravages of time have done to Angela's memories. If symbols had exact, definable values, they would be pointless: the reader could replace them by their known meaning each time he came across them. If, every time we read this novel, we were expected to understand Faith whenever the mountain is mentioned, or Doubt when the snow falls or the wind blows, then the task of reading would be reduced to mechanical deciphering. We must respect the intrinsic mysteriousness of much of *San Manuel Bueno, mártir*.

The second general point is that the emotional values of the symbols arise in the minds of specific characters in specific contexts, and we cannot hope to state these values in the abstract. We must ask who is feeling, or perceiving, the symbols at any point in the text. This is especially important in the case of a novel like *San Manuel Bueno, mártir,* where, despite what critics have said about the importance of the idea of community and shared experience in the novel, there is in fact a very radical division between the characters, some of whom enjoy the illusory consolations of religious faith while some, Manuel and Lázaro, suffer the agonies of knowledge of the truth of life. The mood and viewpoint of these two groups are very different, and they consequently experience the natural world in different ways, so that symbolic features in that world have different values for them. Angela's viewpoint is, in a sense, midway between these two groups, for she has both faith and, yet, knowledge — consequently her standpoint is subtly different from everyone else's.

To take the case of the central symbol in the novel, the lake, it means different things for each of these three groups, and one would be embarrassed to try to isolate one interpretation as its definitive meaning. *Lake*

For Manuel and — eventually — Lázaro, it is clearly dolefully reminiscent of death and oblivion. This is perhaps its chief role in the book in the sense that Manuel and Lázaro are the protagonists and are the repositories of the dominant emotion in the text: despair. Thus their responses to their environment to some extent overwhelm those of the other characters. The lake fascinates both of them because it reminds them of their ultimate fate, and since Manuel is, and Lázaro later becomes, suicidal, they are drawn to it and identified with it. Speaking of the lake, Manuel confesses 'He aquí mi tentación mayor...¡cómo me llama esa agua con su aparente quietud!' (pp. 52-3), and Manuel is associated with the lake at other points:

> ... había en sus ojos toda la hondura azul de nuestro lago. (p. 8)

> — en el fondo del alma de nuestro don Manuel hay también sumergida, ahogada, una villa ... (p. 42, Lázaro speaking)

The same image means different things for different people. eg lake means death + despair for Manuel + Lázaro but for Angela 70, who believes, lake reminds her of the home she loves.

Unamuno: San Manuel Bueno, mártir

After Manuel's death Lázaro is infected with the same death-wish and is equally enticed by the lake: 'se pasaba horas contemplando el lago. Sentía morriña de la paz verdadera' (p. 71).

Nor is it surprising that these two characters should connect the lake with death, since it is reputedly the watery grave of the legendary villagers who have already suffered the fate which they at once both secretly long for and fear.

But the lake does not therefore mean Death in the context of the novel. For other characters of different convictions or dispositions, it means something else. For Angela, a believer (at least until the very end), the lake and the mountain are warm reminders of the home that she loves. In the city, she says, 'me faltaba algo, sentía sed de la vista de las aguas del lago, hambre de la vista de las peñas de la montaña' (p. 33). For her and Lázaro's mother the lake is also something to be loved and contemplated with affection, and not a sinister reminder of oblivion. She is a believer who longs to go to Heaven 'desde donde se viese el lago y la montaña de Valverde de Lucerna' (p. 39), an illusion she shares with the other villagers.

But from the start the lake has other, vague and rather unsettling connotations for Angela — as befits her complex position as a believer who intuits a sad truth. Early in the novel it is she who notices the link between the blue lake and the eyes of Manuel (pp. 8, 32). This happens before she has discovered the truth about Manuel. Her intuition that there is something more to the lake than its nature as the chief feature of the countryside around her beloved village is an indication of the ambivalence of the lake in the text — as well as of her privileged position as the narrator who progresses from ignorance to a state of painful enlightenment.

In fact this ambivalence is most vividly expressed in the image of the drowned village which means different things for Manuel and Lázaro on the one hand, and for a believer on the other. For the former it is a baleful *memento mori*: the truth that life is brief and pointless is submerged in Manuel's soul just as the village is drowned beneath the waters. But for

the uninitiated Angela it is still a reassuring promise of permanence and immortality, for she imagines that in the chiming
of its bells she can hear the 'voz de nuestros muertos que en
nosotros resucitaban en la comunión de los santos' (p. 18).
The lake is thus an ambiguous, even cruel, symbol which
functions in the text by virtue of its contrasting meaning for
those who know the truth and for those who have religious
faith.

It is perhaps in the notions of contrast and paradox that
we come closest to a key to the nature and role of symbols in
San Manuel Bueno, mártir. The disagreements between the
critics described previously probably originate in their tendency
to isolate merely one or two functions of each symbol and to
describe them as the unique attributes of natural objects. Take,
for example, snow in the text of the novel. This has been
declared to symbolize 'human life' by one critic and 'doubt' by
another. But a closer reading reveals that snow does not, in
itself, have an intrinsic symbolic value at all in *San Manuel
Bueno, mártir*. An attentive reading of the scene in which
Manuel is strangely affected by the falling snowflakes indicates
that it is not the snow in itself which elicits his comment, but
the contrast between something disappearing and something
remaining. Manuel's emotional life is based on a struggle
between a will to survive and a longing for death. Consequently,
the surrounding world constantly reflects back to him images
of this paradox, reminders of the conflict between what is
stable and what is ephemeral. The snow vanishing on the lake
disturbs him not because snow is in itself ephemeral, but
precisely because the snow on the mountainside settles and
remains: '¿Has visto, Lázaro, misterio mayor que el de la
nieve cayendo en el lago y muriendo en él mientras cubre con
su toca a la montaña?' (p. 54). It is this contrast which
generates the emotion, so that we might more accurately speak
of a symbolic situation than of a symbolic object. For this
reason it is possible to say that snow is not itself symbolic in
this passage, but rather that the total scene recalls Manuel's
dilemma by its juxtaposition of what is fleeting and what
survives.

It is such contrasts between permanence and flux that underlie many of the most emotively charged passages in the novel. The lake, for example, fascinates Manuel because of the difference between its apparent stillness and its real movement: 'esa agua con su aparente quietud — la corriente va por dentro ...' (p. 53). He is affected by the goatherd singing on the mountainside because of the apparent timelessness of the scene — 'parece como si se hubiera acabado el tiempo' (p. 54) — the ironic and tragic force of the remark resting on the word *parece,* since Manuel knows better than most how quickly time is passing. And it is finally contrast which is the key to the other major symbol in the novel, the mountain. It is not possible to ascribe a fixed symbolic value to the mountain itself because it never appears alone, but always contrasted or compared with the invisibly flowing waters of the lake beside it. Again, it is the total situation which carries the emotional charge, not the object in itself. The mountain is never mentioned in contexts where the lake does not also appear —

> su aldea perdida como un broche entre el lago y la montaña que se mira en él. (p. 13)

> llevaba la cabeza como nuestra peña del Buitre lleva su cresta, y había en sus ojos toda la hondura azul de nuestro lago. (p. 8)

> sed de la vista de las aguas del lago, hambre de la vista de las peñas de la montaña ... (p. 33)

> en el cielo ... desde donde se viese el lago y la montaña ... (p. 39)

> una cabrera, que enhiesta sobre un picacho de la falda de la montaña, a la vista del lago ... (p. 54)

> del lago, a cuya sobrehaz rizaba entonces la brisa montañosa ... (p. 56)

We might, in speaking of the symbol of the mountain, say that it always appears in binary opposition to the lake; and as a consequence, the value of each is dependent on the other.

What this opposition is, is no doubt suggested by the bulk of the towering rock set against the silent waters which are actually flowing into the bitter sea of Death — as we are reminded by Lázaro on page 72. It is the same paradox as that which obsesses Manuel and haunts the whole novel: the conflict between the desire of all human beings to live for ever like the mountain, and the certain knowledge that all will pass into oblivion like the water beneath. Like human existence itself, Valverde de Lucerna is symbolically perched between these two contrasting symbols of mortality and permanence. It is the 'aldea perdida entre el lago y la montaña' (p. 13), facing both ways in the sense that some of its inhabitants know the truth and others fondly believe in the afterlife. Indeed, the mountain is connected with the comforting vanities of religion since it bears the ruins of a monastery whence medieval men once propagated the fiction of a life after death.

Of the other natural feature which recurs in the novel, namely the *cierzo de hostigo* or driving north wind, it may be said that it is not so much itself a symbol as a reminder of the presence of the lake. It is mentioned only twice, and on both occasions the image is of the waters of the lake trembling at the touch of the cold wind. On the first occasion the tremor which passes through the congregation when they hear Manuel/ Jesus's protest to God at being abandoned is like 'un temblor hondo como por sobre las aguas del lago en días de cierzo de hostigo' (p. 16). On the other occasion, Manuel's trembling on handing Lázaro the Host at Communion is also compared to the same phenomenon (p. 43). Both images are evoked by the power of the human emotions aroused by a reminder of the desolateness of the human condition. Nor is the *cierzo* merely a wind: it is cold and pitiless, and Unamuno's use of such images reminds us just how pessimistic, even desperate, is the basic vision of the novel. The icy gale ripples the lake which contains the drowned village and also Manuel's dream of suicide and oblivion.

It would be possible to speculate endlessly about these various images, but the important thing is that they should deliver their emotional charge to the reader by a process of

suggestion. It is of the nature of effective literary symbols not
to be reducible to dry intellectual concepts, and when a text
depends as much on mysteries, secrets and echoes as does this
novel, nothing is gained by dispelling the vagueness and re-
placing it with a concreteness devoid of poetic force. There
is, moreover, a sense in which it is superfluous to talk of
symbols in *San Manuel Bueno, mártir,* since the whole text
functions symbolically. This point was made in Chapters 3 and
4 where it was noted that the village, the characters, the
language and the plot itself were deliberately dissociated from
any specific time or place except the Holy Lands. As a result
of these rather successful attempts of Unamuno's to introduce
a certain degree of mystification into his text, it is perfectly
permissible to see allusions to universal notions like Death,
Faith, Eternity and God at every point in the novel. The text
is designed to invite this kind of speculation by virtue of its
very openness. It is only necessary to remind oneself that one
is speculating rather than discovering the author's intentions.
The latter, as so often with Unamuno, were to generate
uncertainties and open up emotional possibilities in the reader,
not to settle his doubts or terminate his enquiries with definite
answers.

7. *Conclusion: the novel and the critics*

I<small>N</small> 'Almas sencillas' (*OC,* X, pp. 991-4) Unamuno recalls how he received a letter from a class of foreign students of Spanish asking him if one of his female characters (Julia in *Nada menos que todo un hombre*) really did grant her favours to one of the men in the novel. He comments that he was delighted to see that he has managed to make a fiction *(ensueño)* so lifelike that readers have become psychologically curious about it; but he replied to the students that he had been unable to find out more facts than those that appear in the text. It is not the author, he continues, who knows his characters best, and when asked by another reader why a certain character said something, he could only reply that he had no idea (p. 992). It is, he concludes, a sad example of aesthetic ignorance to imagine that an author speaks through his *criaturas.*

Most critics (Shaw, *5,* is a notable exception) ignore this argument, and assume that *San Manuel Bueno, mártir* is not so much a novel as disguised autobiography. Despite all the fictionalizing devices and disclaimers, and despite all the disagreements between Unamuno's own views and the text, they cheerfully assert, sometimes on the most preposterous evidence, that Manuel Bueno is merely the real Unamuno thinly disguised. Fernández claims that the novel's *autobiografismo* is 'total', even down to what this critic manages to persuade himself is the obvious similarity of names between Miguel de Unamuno and Manuel Bueno. . . . [1] Sánchez Barbudo asserts that 'en ningún pasaje se pintó él tan esencialmente como en ese cura' (*14,* p. 151). Basdekis states that the text is 'an

---

[1] *Unamuno en su espejo* (Valencia, 1975), p. 216.

autobiographical novelization of Unamuno's "tragic sense of life" ' (*19,* p. 78), and Regalado García calls it 'una autobiografía del espíritu de su creador que incluye en ella su posición final ante los transcendentales problemas que le inquietaron y le justificaron su vida' (*13,* pp. 202-8).

Unamuno, who constantly said (in passages so numerous that one marvels that they are never taken seriously) that it would be impossible to define his final position, would have been indignant about these assumptions of identity between him and his creatures. One neglected consequence of the autobiographical fallacy is the covert (in Regalado García's case, explicit) value judgement that the worth of the novel derives from its long overdue sincerity: it lets us know at last what Unamuno really thought about Christianity and death. But what does this value judgement tell us about his other works? Are *Del sentimiento trágico de la vida, Paz en la guerra, Abel Sánchez,* insincere and merely provisional? Was the Unamuno who harangued the republican crowds from the balcony in April 1931 simply a fraud? Why is one type of emotion, the apolitical pessimism of this novel, to be valued as authentic in contrast to another type which is dismissed as counterfeit? And why should a book written in one's sixty-fifth year be a truer statement of one's deepest lifelong convictions than a book written, like *La agonía del cristianismo,* in one's sixtieth year? The fact is that to praise *San Manuel Bueno, mártir* as revealing autobiography raises numerous methodological problems, and it is to fail to judge the work as literature. It also implies a negative judgement of Unamuno's earlier works.

The assumption that the novel is an accurate confession of Unamuno's own beliefs lets in all kinds of extra-literary arguments which replace critical discussion of the text. Once one assumes that it is a political or religious manifesto one will inevitably write political or theological criticism about it.

Left-wingers, for example, have seen the novel as a reactionary document written by a deplorable enemy of the people. The first critic so to condemn Unamuno (though without specific reference to this novel) was probably the Communist

A. Bazán in *Unamuno y el marxismo* (Madrid, 1935), and in the preface to this work, the Soviet critic Ilya Ehrenburg condemned Unamuno for not protesting about the real conditions of the real villagers in the squalid hamlets on the shores of the lake of Sanabria. (An unfair accusation: Unamuno did protest in the 1933 prologue to the novel.)

Regalado García also attacks the novel from an apparently left-wing position. By attributing Manuel's duplicity about Christianity to Unamuno, he takes the author to task for wanting to create a medieval Spain which would be a supportive environment for the religious faith he so desperately yearns for. Manuel eliminates the progressive Lázaro as an obstacle to these plans: the latter's conversion is a 'chantaje espiritual'. In the novel the author 'proyecta una filosofía política' which envisages a totalitarian state in which Manuel is the dictator (*13*, pp. 202-8).

Even the excellent socialist political scientist Elías Díaz raids the novel for evidence of Unamuno's essential conservatism. For him, Manuel's dismissal of the agrarian syndicate is proof of the author's tendency to underestimate concrete human problems like the unequal distribution of wealth, and of his 'indiferencia irracional' to human welfare (*9*, p. 16).

These left-wing complaints can be swiftly dealt with. Let us allow for the sake of argument that Manuel Bueno is a reactionary (although this is very doubtful: *pace* Regalado García, he does not try to prevent the foundation of an agrarian syndicate but merely does not care about it: 'que jueguen al sindicato, si eso les contenta', hardly the remark of an obstructive conservative). But this does not mean that the novel itself is reactionary. One cannot derive the meaning of a text from the meaning of the utterances of its main character — to do so is to ignore the role of irony. If Unamuno agreed with Manuel, would he have written this novel? If it were a straightforward tract preaching piety and resignation in the poor, the evils of social change and the eternal truth of Catholic dogmas, then we might reasonably call it anti-progressive. But this novel is the opposite of that. It shows an ordained priest pretending to have faith and thus subverts the whole notion of the infallibility of the Church in a few pages. In the act of publishing such a text Unamuno surely makes the hold of religion and tradition on his readers' minds weaker, not stronger. We, as readers, are denied the solace of the villagers, because like Angela we learn the awful truth. Unlike Manuel, Unamuno is not trying to fool us. Such a literary project is hardly the work of a conventional political or religious reactionary.

The paradox is that Unamuno, who certainly envied the faith of convinced Catholics, also wrote works which tended to undermine it, and this ambiguity in the political or religious message of the novel is displayed by the fact that some critics have taken the view that, far from being a conservative, traditionalist text, it is a blatant denunciation of Catholicism and all its works. Gullón finds it to be an attack on the Church and on religion itself: 'no sería difícil intentar una explicación de *San Manuel Bueno* como ataque decisivo y final de Unamuno contra la Iglesia; más aún, contra la religión' (*20,* p. 336), a reading which demands that we take Manuel to be a scoundrel whose deceits are utterly immoral. But there is nothing in the text to justify such a conclusion, nor was it typical of Unamuno — as we have seen — to condemn Christianity either by his words or by his actions. If the novel has a message about religion, and its ambiguities are such that one hesitates to pronounce finally on the matter, it is surely that some men believe religious faith is better than knowledge of the truth, and that given the miseries of existence one can hardly blame them for thinking so. The text does not seem to be more conclusive than this, although the statement is more than suggestive enough to make the novel a profoundly disturbing work. Sánchez Barbudo does not consider the novel itself to be anticlerical, but he does read it as incontrovertible proof of Unamuno's 'completa falta de fe' (*14,* p. 142).

Sánchez Barbudo's study of the text is the best general introduction to *San Manuel Bueno, mártir,* but it is not, ultimately, about the novel so much as about its author. Chapter 4 of this guide was addressed to the problems raised by taking the novel as a straight statement of its author's beliefs: there are no real grounds for assuming that Manuel Bueno's absolute incapacity to believe in an afterlife is the same as Unamuno's own agonizing doubts about the problem. The fact that a writer creates a character who cannot believe does not therefore necessarily amount to a declaration that his unbelief is well-founded. Need we attribute Manuel's attitude to Unamuno? It is not reasonable to read fiction as though it were autobiographical fact. Moreover, the statement that God does not exist is never made in the novel.

Blanco Aguinaga rightly complains that hardly any *Unamunistas* have practised literary criticism on the text, but have instead used it as a source of statements about extra-textual matters like Unamuno's own state of mind or his philosophical ideas. In an article which adopts a position close to this guide he insists on the complexity of the relationship between the novel and its author (22). The novel does not invite firm conclusions about the problems it raises. The events are mediated via a fictional narrator's memories of her fictional brother's account of Manuel, and we cannot grasp the real facts through the fog of these memories. Consequently, it is a 'novela enigma en la que, quizá por primera vez, logra Unamuno creer un mundo libre, ficción en la cual los contrarios se cruzan y se funden dejando al lector sin ningún sostén conceptual definido...'.

This is a much overdue emphasis on the autonomous literary status of the text; on the qualities of ambiguity and polyvalence which make it into literature rather than biography or social documentary. Unamuno's personality is so powerful, and it looms so large over everything he wrote, that it is difficult to avoid reducing all discussion of his literary works to discussions about his character or beliefs. But he made unusual efforts in this novel to detach himself from the views of his protagonist, and to obscure the degree of his own commitment to Manuel's desperate philosophy. As a result, *San Manuel Bueno, mártir* has an elusive quality: it hints very broadly at a major statement about the nature of religion, especially of Christianity, but it does so obliquely, in such a way that we cannot be sure that the author himself takes such a pessimistic view as his defeatist hero who really believes that the pursuit of truth brings nothing but despair and anguish.

It is thus appropriate to end this study on a deliberately inconclusive note. The temptation is strong to conclude guides such as these with some magisterial utterance about the ultimate significance or value of the text in question, but throughout the previous pages an effort has been made to show why this is impossible in this case. Unamuno's work in general, and this novel in particular, will not yield a single, concrete meaning. One has only to survey the products of Unamuno studies to see this. Some critics find the novel to be reactionary and authoritarian; others find it to be subversive, atheistic, even anti-clerical. Some find it to be an apology for the repression of the masses; others have found it to be a plea for tolerance in the face of the polarization of society after the fall of Alfonso XIII. For some critics, particularly those given to elucubrations about the so-called modern crisis, it is a classic of existentialism and therefore very close to the heart of the central problems of our times. Others, humanists and rationalists, deplore its tendency to value myth and tradition over independent thought. For some it is an appeal for authenticity, for others it is a defence of blatant *mauvaise foi,* the work of a man who has lost interest in the future of mankind. This constant shifting of assessments tells us much about the ideological basis of most critical judgements, but it also dramatically reveals the bizarre Janus face of most of Unamuno's work, which constitutes both a position and its own denial, a sort of two-sided argument in which the real Unamuno was ultimately impartial or undecided. Virtually none of the positions adopted by *Unamunistas* is wrong, and most are supported by massive and accurate quotation from the author's works: it is rather that they pick out facets from a whole which is almost too complex to encompass.

Nor is it in the nature of Unamuno's novels to provide us with many clues about their definitive conclusions. They generally raise dilemmas which admit of no solutions, and leave the reader to cope as best he can. In the case of this novel, the questions raised are truly massive for so short a

work. Are comforting lies preferable to painful truths? Is the
function of all religion, specifically of Christianity, to deceive
us into believing life has a meaning? Do some men, especially
Jesus himself, willingly face death in order to underwrite myths
in which they do not themselves believe, motivated by love of
their fellow men and the conviction that the best gift one can
bestow on humanity is a fairy tale of human hope? Is such
deception a moral act? The text of the novel does not decide
these awesome questions, and a sensitive reading merely asks
that we feel the force of them and be troubled by them. This
is what Unamuno would have wanted.

Bibliographical note

EDITIONS

1 The *Obras completas,* 16 vols (Madrid: Afrodisio Aguado, 1958-64), and the less disorganized Escelicer edition (Madrid, 1966-in progress), both edited by Manuel García Blanco, provide the only convenient access to the bulk of Unamuno's work.

2 The Austral edition of *SMB, San Manuel Bueno, mártir y tres historias más* (Buenos Aires: Espasa-Calpe, 1942), is a faithful version of the 1933 edition.

3 Mario J. and María Elena Valdés's *Comparative and Critical Edition of 'San Manuel Bueno, mártir',* Estudios de Hispanófila, no. 27 (Chapel Hill, 1973) is a carefully prepared edition with English translation. However the chapter numbers are the editors' own invention.

BIOGRAPHY

4 Salcedo, Emilio, *Vida de don Miguel,* 2nd ed. (Salamanca: Anaya, 1970) is excellent — though sometimes inaccurate on details for Unamuno's life before 1900.

GENERAL STUDIES

5 The best introduction to Unamuno is perhaps the brief account in Donald L. Shaw, *The Generation of 1898 in Spain* (London: Benn, 1975), pp. 41-74.

6 Barea, Arturo, *Unamuno* (Cambridge: Bowes and Bowes, 1952) is a useful short introduction.

7 Nozick, Martin, *Miguel de Unamuno,* Twayne's World Authors Series, 175 (New York: Twayne, 1969) is also recommended as a short introduction.

8 Blanco Aguinaga, Carlos, *El Unamuno contemplativo* (Mexico City: El Colegio de México, 1959) draws attention to the 'other'

Unamuno who was attracted to silence and oblivion. It provides much detailed information about the defeatist and escapist feelings which no doubt partly inform *San Manuel Bueno, mártir*.

9 Díaz, Elías, *El pensamiento político de Unamuno* (Madrid: Tecnos, 1965), is a useful anthology of Unamuno's political writings compiled by a critical but fair-minded socialist scholar.

10 González Martín, Vicente, editor, *República española y España republicana (1931-1936)* (Salamanca: Almar, 1979) is an invaluable anthology of Unamuno's contradictory reactions to the Second Republic.

11 Marías, Julián, *Miguel de Unamuno* (Buenos Aires: Emecé, 1942), is a philosophical but jargon-free account of Unamuno's thought.

12 Marrero, Vicente, *El Cristo de Unamuno* (Madrid: Rialp, 1960), a Catholic critique of Unamuno's heterodox ideas which contains much revealing material.

13 Regalado García, Antonio, *El siervo y el señor* (Madrid: Gredos, 1968), a provocative, often very subjective left-wing account of Unamuno's work.

14 Sánchez Barbudo, Antonio, *Estudios sobre Unamuno y Machado* (Madrid: Guadarrama, 1959), is a mine of information about Unamuno in general and the background to *San Manuel Bueno* in particular.

15 Zubizarreta, Armando F., *Unamuno en su nivola* (Madrid: Taurus, 1960) contains a long and often subjective account of the crisis Unamuno suffered in the mid 1920s.

16 Zubizarreta, Armando F., *Tras las huellas de Unamuno* (Madrid: Taurus, 1960), contains much interesting information on Unamuno's formative years — but beware the heavy Catholic bias, which presents the crisis of 1897 as a conversion.

ON UNAMUNO'S NOVELS

17 Batchelor, R. E., *Unamuno Novelist: a European Perspective* (Oxford: Dolphin, 1972), finds echoes of Unamuno in much of European literature, but contains useful insights.

18 Díez, Ricardo, *El desarrollo estético de la novela de Unamuno* (Madrid: Playor, 1976).

19 Basdekis, Demetrius, *Unamuno and the Novel*, Estudios de Hispanófila, no. 31 (Chapel Hill, 1974).

20 Gullón, Ricardo, *Autobiografías de Unamuno* (Madrid: Gredos, 1964), an interesting and readable study.

21 Turner, David G., *Unamuno's Webs of Fatality* (London: Tamesis, 1974) is the best and most comprehensive book about Unamuno's novels.

ON 'SAN MANUEL BUENO, MÁRTIR'

22 Blanco Aguinaga, Carlos, 'Sobre la complejidad de *San Manuel Bueno, mártir,* novela' in *Miguel de Unamuno,* edited by A. Sánchez Barbudo (Madrid: Taurus, 1974), pp. 273-96, adopts, in rather technical language, a position close to this study.

23 Falconieri, John V., *'San Manuel Bueno, mártir* — Spiritual Autobiography: a Study in Imagery', *Symposium,* XVIII (1964), 128-41.

24 Fernández, Pelayo H., *El problema de la personalidad en Unamuno y en San Manuel Bueno* (Madrid, 1966), a highly impressionistic account.